THE NORTH SHORE OF
LAKE
SUPERIOR
Yesterday and Today

Dr. Duane R. Lund

Distributed by
Adventure Publications
P. O. Box 269
Cambridge, Minnesota 55008

ISBN 0-934860-01-7

Dedication

*To the late Ted Tofte — distinguished
educator and friend who shared with me
so many stories about growing up on the
North Shore of Lake Superior.*

TABLE OF CONTENTS

CHAPTER I
THE
GREAT WATER ROAD

The Ojibway called it "Kitchi-gumi". The French called it "Grand Lac". Both mean "big lake", a name that is surely appropriate:

The largest of the five Great Lakes.

The largest body of freshwater in the world[1] — containing 10% of the world's supply.

More than 350 miles of water between Duluth-Superior and Sault Ste. Marie, and 1,826 miles of shoreline.

It is a virtual freshwater ocean.

Lake Superior has been characterized as being "like the Himalayas among mountains or the Amazon among rivers".[2]

The lake is incredibly deep, 1,333 feet in one place[3] — and cold,[4] crystal clear water. And the surrounding landscape is stunning—rocky palisades and gorgeous timber of many varieties: towering white and Norway pines, majestic spruce, sturdy oaks, golden aspen and red maples whose autumn fire is unexcelled, even in New England. Lake Superior is like a gigantic precious gem in the center of our continent.

The spectacular beauty of Lake Superior is only a part of the story. Of equal, or perhaps greater, importance is its incredible value to mankind over thousands of years. The lake and its almost countless streams have been a cornucopia of fish of all varieties and its shores have provided habitat for game and fur-bearing animals of all descriptions. It fed and clothed those people who lived on its shores for more than 100 generations. It was Lake Superior's copper mines that gave the Native Americans their first metal tools, spears, hooks, gaffs, and other implements. Some archeologists believe that the copper artifacts found in burial sites near here are the first metal instruments used in either North or South America. Perhaps most important, however, is the great water road the lake provided. It is the longest link in the historic east-west transcontinental water highway.

For thousands of years before the huge ore boats began to ply its expansive waters, Lake Superior served as the western terminus of the Great Lakes-St. Lawrence River waterway that linked the east coast of North America with the center of the continent. And with the help of numerous portages, starting at either Thunder Bay or Grand Portage, the lake became a springboard for expeditions — mostly by water — as far as Lake Athabasca, two-thirds of the way west across the continent, or north via the Boundary Waters to the Lake of the Woods and up the Winnipeg and Nelson Rivers to Hudson's Bay. There was also fairly easy access to the Mississippi River and the lakes of what is now northern Minnesota at Fond du Lac (now Duluth-Superior) via the St. Louis River and the Savannah Portage to Sandy Lake and from there to that mighty river, which has been the chief north-south waterway of the continent. It is little wonder Lake Superior is so rich in history!

We really don't know when the first people arrived in North America. We believe they came from Asia and that they probably came across the Bering Straits to what we now call Alaska. Some archeologists say they first migrated south along the Pacific coast before exploring east and eventually crossing the continent. There is a pretty good possibility those first North Americans journeyed east by way of Lake Superior. Travel by land was extremely difficult so waterways were used as much as possible. No doubt the tributaries of the Mississippi were also used on the west to east migrations but the going would have been a whole lot slower once the migrants ran out of water routes.

We do know that by the time the first white explorers discovered the Great Lakes they found their shores held many Indian village sites and the lakes were extensively used for travel. Although some Indian tribes were nomadic and changed village locations fairly frequently, there were other tribes which lived on the same sites for many generations. Yet, even these people traveled a good deal as they hunted, trapped, went on raids, or just explored — perhaps more out of curiosity than need. For example, we know that when the Hudson's Bay Company first located on the bay from which it took its name, Indians were willing to bring their furs from at least as far away as Minnesota to exchange them for trade goods. Of course, this was prior to the coming of the independent traders and the North West Company to the Boundary Waters. We also have records of Leech Lake Indians traveling as far as Mackinac.[5] And John Tanner, hero of *White Indian Boy* by this author, was kidnapped in Kentucky by Shawnee Indians and brought to their village on the Maunee River — more than a 10 day journey. There he was purchased by a traveling Ottawa family with roots in modern day Manitoba, and they returned there by way of Lake

Superior. We also know that war parties thought nothing of raiding villages one, or even two, hundred miles away.

With so much travel by the Indian peoples, it is probably safe to assume that in spite of the dangers of the big waters, Lake Superior was heavily used for travel from the very beginning of mankind's coming to this part of North America.

Geologists tell us that before there was a Lake Superior, this part of the continent was covered with a thick layer of molten rock — a basalt more than one mile thick in places — that poured out of the earth's bowels through a rift in the crust. The Sawtooth Mountains along the North Shore are thought to be the well-worn remains of ancient volcanoes. Evidence of lava flows may be found at a number of places in the area including Gooseberry Falls and Carlton Peak (near Tofte).

Geologists hypothesize that the area was long arid — but then came the build up of glaciers (four in all). As each receded, it scraped rock against rock, like a giant bulldozer, thereby shaping the lake and the surrounding area. And melting glaciers meant water — lots of water!

One can only imagine what Lake Superior was like during prehistoric times. Although the lake itself is probably much like it was not long after the last glacier receded, the animal life of today is indeed different. We can be quite certain those earliest residents were contemporary with the woolly mammoth because artifacts made of "live ivory" have been found in burial mounds in the general region. And a species of beaver existed which was very much larger than the present day variety. There was also a giant bison. As recent as the 1600s, Radisson wrote of seeing buffalo and elk in this general area. There have been some changes in the animal life even in this century. In the early 1900s, for example, there was an abundance of moose and bear, but fewer deer. However, there were woodland caribou along the shore and there was even a season for hunting them in Minnesota as late as 1906[6].

Although some archeologists believe that Indian peoples traveled and lived on Lake Superior from shortly after the receding of the last glacier (eight to ten thousand years ago)[7] we really know practically nothing about the first several thousands of years of inhabitation.

When we realize that the involvement of white people on Lake Superior is only about 5% of human history on the lake, we get some perspective of how much history is unknown. Yet, these hundreds of generations of people no doubt were very much like us. They had to work to feed and clothe themselves. They sometimes had to fight to the death to protect their territory and their way of life. But they had time for fun and games, too, and no doubt laughed and loved just as we do today.

Earliest Peoples

The first people in this area who have been identified with a name lived to the west of Lake Superior. We classify them as a separate tribe because their burial mounds are so unique. They are, in fact, huge — some nearly 40 feet high and 100 feet in length. Archeologists believe they were used to bury several generations of people who lived near those sites. Although none of these huge mounds is found by Lake

Prehistoric mound, at Mound Park, near Laurel, Minn. Height 28 ft. Width 115 ft. One of the largest mounds found built by the Prehistoric Race, called "Mound Builders".

Superior, they are found in the nearby Boundary Waters. In 1844, George Bryce[8] reported 24 of these larger mounds along the Rainy River. There are five mounds on the American side at the mouth of the Big Fork River at Laurel. Archeologists used this name in identifying the tribe; they called them "the Laurel Culture". They have also been called "the Mound Builders". Although they may not have lived on Lake Superior, they were so close they no doubt were on the lake from time to time. We can be quite certain the copper artifacts found in their mounds came from copper sources on Lake Superior — probably Isle Royale.

The Laurel were a most interesting people. Their burial mounds contained ornaments from shells which could only have come from the Pacific or the Gulf of Mexico. Their skeletal remains indicate that they were about the size of modern man. It is believed they came here sometime around the birth of Christ — a time when people were considerably shorter than we are today, possibly making them relative giants for their time. They also had some unusual burial customs. The bones were buried in bundles, indicating that the bodies were probably placed in trees or on scaffolds where they were allowed to decompose before burial. The marrow was removed from the larger bones and the brains removed from some of the skulls soon after

Birchbark canoes under construction.

death. In some cases the eye sockets were filled with clay. Archeologists also believe they may have been the first Indians to bring the bow and arrow to this part of the continent.

Sometime around 1000 A.D., a new people entered the northern region; they have been called the Blackduck Culture.[9] From their burial mounds, archeologists have concluded that they lived pretty much as the Indian peoples found in this area by the first white explorers. The Laurel people may have left, been driven out or died out by the time the Blackducks arrived. They just disappeared. It is possible, of course, that they were assimilated by the Blackduck people.

It was also about 1000 A.D. when the Mississippi Culture moved into the area we now know as Minnesota and Wisconsin. They included several of the Sioux tribes and came from the south and west. Gradually they pushed the woodland Indians farther and farther north until by 1600 they occupied all but the extreme northern parts of Minnesota. Their domain included Sandy Lake, Leech Lake and the Red Lakes. Although we do not believe they had permanent villages on the North Shore, they surely had access to Lake Superior at Fond du Lac, Grand Portage and Thunder Bay. In fact, the Thunder Bay (Kaministiquia River) route was originally called "the Old Sioux Trail". These were the Dakota-Sioux.[10] Another Sioux tribe, the Assiniboines, had originally moved into southern Wisconsin. They did not get along well with their Sioux cousins, the Winnebagos, who finally chased them north. The Assiniboine migrated along Lake Superior on their way to what is now called Manitoba. They may have lived along the lake for awhile.

It was about this time that the Europeans were colonizing the east coast of what is now Canada and the United States. The Indian tribes along the coast included the Iroquois Nation (eight tribes)[11] and the Algonquin Nation (eleven tribes).[12] The two Indian nations were traditional enemies. The Iroquois were the first to trade with the whites for guns and powder. With this average, they drove the Algonquins, including the huge Ojibway Nation out of that region. Reportedly thousands were killed. The Ojibway then migrated west along both the south and the north sides of the Great Lakes. At the outset, they apparently had little confrontation with the Dakota-Sioux who by then (1660) had fully occupied the Dakotas, part of Wisconsin and all but the northernmost parts of Minnesota.

This, then was the setting that greeted the first white explorers, traders, and missionaries as they arrived at the west end of Lake Superior in the 17th century.

[1]Lake Baikal in Siberia is much deeper and therefore has a greater volume of water, but its surface area is not as large as Lake Superior.

[2]James Baker in an address to the Minnesota Historical Society, January 24, 1879.

[3]Some of the deepest water (over 1,000 feet) is in a channel that follows nearly all of the North Shore — usually starting just a mile or two out from the shoreline.

[4]Averaging 40° F.

[5]For further information about the Pillager Indians of Leech Lake, consult *Tales of Four Lakes and a River* by this author.

[6]There have been occasional caribou sightings in recent years and some have suggested re-stocking them in the area.

[7]Most archeologists are confident that people were on the lake at least 5,000 years ago.

[8]Bryce, George. *The Lake of the Woods, its History, Geology, etc.* Toronto Free Press, 1897.

[9]Historians have labeled both the Blackduck and Laurel Indians as Woodland Cultures.

[10]There were seven councils of the Dakota-Sioux: Sisseton, Teton, Yankton, Yanktonai, Wahpeton, Wahpakute and Mdewakanton. Other Sioux tribes included the Iowa, Oto, Missouri, Omaha, Osage, Ponca, Hidatsa, Crow, Mandan, Assiniboine and Winnebago.

[11]The Algonquin tribes included the Ojibway (Chippewa), Ottawa, Sac, Fox, Patawatomi, Illinois, Shawnee, Miami, Kickapoo, Menominees, and Cree.

[12]The Iroquois included the Mohawk, Oneida, Onondaga, Cayuga, Seneca, Tuscarora, Erie and the Hurons.

CHAPTER II
EXPLORERS, TRADERS AND MISSIONARIES

Why did they come? Surely there was enough undeveloped country along the Eastern Seaboard to explore and develop. After all, the United States wouldn't even exist for another hundred years and Canada wouldn't be independent for longer than that.

The reason the explorers came so far into the continent in the 1600s — and the traders too — was basically economics. For the nations of Europe, trade was a lucrative business. The silver and gold of South and Central America had already enriched the coffers of the crowned heads of Europe and preliminary reports from the Orient led them to believe even greater treasures, including spices, lay in store in the Far East. The problem was that the eastern route to the Orient from Europe was so long. They thought it might be shorter to go across the Atlantic and then the Pacific. But to reach the Pacific, ships had to make the long and sometimes hazardous journey around the southern tip of South America. What the explorers were seeking was a shortcut across North America or a northwest passage over the continent. They were constantly encouraged by Indians who told of salt water "not many days' journey". As we study the journals of the explorers, we might suspect that some of the Indians were playing games and told them whatever they thought they wanted to hear!

Meanwhile, fur had become the most popular garment in Europe. Originally the clothing of royalty, the great resources of fur-bearing animals of North America made this symbol of success available to anyone who had money. Soon, anybody who was anybody wore furs. Thus there was a rapidly growing market in Europe.

Amazingly, by the 1700s, the convenient streams of our east coast were already being trapped out. Thus, trading and exploring went hand in hand. European governments and merchants, as well as east coast entrepreneurs, were willing to finance explorers only if they paid their way by bringing back precious metals or stones or furs. Explorers who kept journals, such as Pierre La Vérendrye, recorded their frustration at having to spend so much time away from their first love — exploration — to trade with the Indians. The Indians, however, were willing traders. They were eager to exchange relatively easily acquired furs for guns, shot, powder, metal traps, cloth, blankets, ornamental beads, rum, cooking utensils, needles, tools, etc. etc. Thus the traders followed the explorers and soon trading posts, often in the form of forts, were established across the North American wilderness. The first wave of trade expansion was on the rivers and streams flowing into the Great Lakes, starting with Lake Ontario and working west, eventually reaching Lake Superior. It then spread west of Superior via Thunder Bay (Kaministiquia River route) and Grand Portage. Exploration and trade also spread south and west of the lake through Fond du Lac (Duluth).

As we shall see in the next chapter, hundreds of voyageurs were hired to service the trading posts, eventually as far west as Lake Athabasca, nearly 3,000 miles from Montreal.

First Whites on Lake Superior

We have already pointed out that known white presence on Lake Superior is only about five percent of human history on the lake. But who was first after the Native Americans?

The discovery of the Kennsington Runestone in 1898[1], near the city of that name in Minnesota, spurred speculation that the Vikings had not only preceded Columbus in the discovery of this continent but had even traveled inland, possibly via the Great Lakes, at least as far as present day Minnesota in 1362.

William Warren, the noted Indian author of *The History of the Ojibways*, noted that in his efforts to tell the Indians about Christianity, he found they already knew many of the stories of the Old Testament (and not just the great flood which is a part of the traditions of so many cultures). He speculated that the Indian peoples could be one of the lost tribes of Israel. This theory is also held by many of the Mormon faith. And there are similarities between the Hebrew and Indian syntax.

Pierre La Vérendrye, while at Fort St. Charles on the Lake of the Woods, heard about the "white Indians" called "the Mandans". By the descriptions he had heard from the Indians who had visited their villages on the Missouri River, he was almost sure they were a band of lost Frenchmen. When he was finally able to visit their villages near present day Mandan,[2] North Dakota, he was quite disappointed. He concluded they were of European origin, all right, because of their physical appearance. Some had light skin, blue eyes, and blond or red hair. The men also treated the women differently than did other Indian men. They worked alongside them in their gardens and the men and women walked side by side; not woman behind the man as was the custom in many tribes. The villages were also European in their design. They had walls around them; some had moats; and the house-like structures within were arranged as though located on streets. La Vérendrye concluded, however, that they just couldn't be of French origin because no self-respecting Frenchman would sleep naked–as did the Mandans!

Unfortunately, most of the Mandans, and apparently all of the light-complected, were wiped out by the smallpox plague of 1782. Later explorers, such as Lewis and Clark, arrived too late to see the white Indians firsthand, but they were able to verify stories of their existence.

Another piece of evidence supporting pre-Columbian explorations by whites inland on North America is a grave unearthed near Thunder Bay containing a sword, axes and the remains of a shield or drum — possibly a Viking.

Before we leave this subject of earliest white visitors to Lake Superior, there is another story just too interesting to not mention here. Peter Kalm, a Swedish traveler and author who admired and talked with Pierre La Vérendrye, told about an object La Vérendrye said he picked up in his travels. It was described as rock with writing on it in an unknown language. It was reportedly about one foot in length and four or five inches wide. It was fixed on a pillar and La Vérendrye's men supposedly broke it off. La Vérendrye also told Kalm of other such pillars found here and there in the wilderness, but without rocks with inscriptions. The stone with writing on it was brought back east by La Vérendrye and given to the Jesuits. They reportedly thought the letters to be Tartaric. Present day language experts point out that Tartaric letters are very much like the runic letters of the early Scandinavians. Interesting! It should be noted that La Vérendrye does not refer to this stone in the journals this author has read, but some of his journals are missing and the reference could be in them.

Who, then, were the first whites on Lake Superior? We probably will never know. We do know, however, that the Jesuits recorded visits of their missionaries to what later was to be called Sault Ste. Marie as early as 1612 — and that will have to do for now.

Brule and Grenoble — 1620s

Champlain, in his writings, talks about Lake Superior. In the early 1620s he sent Brule and an interpreter named Grenoble to live among the Indians of the western wilderness. They may have been at least as far west as Isle Royale, because they described their visits to native-operated copper mines. Of course, this could have been on the south shore. Based on their descriptions and later reports, Champlain published a map of Lake Superior in 1665; he called it "Grand Lac".

Fathers Joques and Ramibault — 1641

The two priests visited the rapids between Lakes Huron and Superior in 1641 and named them Sault Ste. Marie in honor of the Virgin Mary.

Radisson and Groseilliers — 1650s

Radisson and Groseilliers were French and they were brothers-in-law. They wanted to form a trading company and asked their own government for financial help. It was denied. They then turned to the British government and received both encouragement and support from King Charles I. The King issued an official charter of incorporation on May 2, 1670.[3]

Prior to receiving this authorization, the men spent several years exploring the North American wilderness from Hudson's Bay south. It is sometimes difficult to tell from their journals just where they traveled, but some believe they may have been the first to operate a trading post at the mouth of the Kaministiquia River, at or near the site where Fort William later appeared. Supposedly this was sometime between 1654 and 1656. We do know that in later years they were at Grand Portage and on the Boundary Waters. In fact, the Pigeon River was originally named for Groseilliers. The English had difficulty pronouncing his name so they used "gooseberry" instead! They called Radisson, "radish". Early maps also gave his name to other rivers on the North Shore, including present day Gooseberry River and Falls. We also know from Radisson's journals that in 1660 they built a cabin on the south shore, probably Chequamegon Bay, near Madeline Island. That same year their journeys took them into Wisconsin and possibly into Minnesota. A pretty good case can be made that they explored as far as Knife Lake, near Mora, where they held a conclave with the Dakota-Sioux. At the end of that journey, they returned east with canoes laden with furs, causing great interest in the Lake Superior area on the part of traders and merchants.

Duluth — 1678

David Greysolon, the sieur du Lhut, was among the first whites to establish trading operations on the north shore of Lake Superior, probably at Grand Portage, Nipigon Bay, Thunder Bay and Fond du Lac. His post at the mouth of the Kaministiquia River was called Fort Caministigogan. He wintered with the Ojibway and the French traders at Sault Ste. Marie in 1678-'79. The French and Ojibway got along very well; they had formed an alliance against their common enemies—the

British and the Iroquois. In the spring of 1679, Duluth journeyed to the western end of the Lake, bringing a number of Ojibway with him. It was then that he established as least one of his trading posts.

You will recall from our first chapter that in the 1640s the Ojibway (and other Algonquin tribes) were driven away from their ancestral homes along the east coast by the Iroquois. They were forced to move west and they migrated along both the south and north shores of the Great Lakes. Sault Ste. Marie became their first major village and capital. Missionaries who visited the site in 1640 estimated the population at about 2,000. Later in the century the Ojibway migrated farther west as most left Sault Ste. Marie, and established a new headquarters at La Pointe[4] (by Madeline Island) with a peak population of about 1,000. These were really large villages when we take into account that the entire Indian population (all tribes combined) in what we now call Minnesota was estimated at 20,000 when the first white men came.

Up until Duluth's arrival, there had been relatively little hostility between the Sioux and the Ojibway, but the Sioux must surely have been wondering about their new neighbors, as well armed as they were with muzzleloaders.

Duluth and the other French traders knew that if the Indian tribes were at war there would be little opportunity for trade. For this reason, later in 1679, Duluth arranged for an historic conclave of Indian tribes residing within a radius of more than 200 miles. The meeting took place at a location he described as "Fond du Lac", the end of the lake, at or near the site of the city that now bears his name. The Assiniboine came from what is now Manitoba; the Dakota-Sioux from what is now North and South Dakota and most of Minnesota; and the Cree came from extreme northern Minnesota and what is now called Northwest Ontario. Duluth brought representatives of the Ojibway with him. All pledged to cooperate and trade in peace with the French. No mean accomplishment! And the arrangement held together pretty well for more than 50 years. The role of the Ojibway was to act as middlemen between the Indians and the handful of French traders. In a sense, the Ojibway were the original voyageurs. La Salle reported that the Ojibway were trading with the Sioux during this period as far as 150 miles west of the Mississippi. Thus, Duluth[5] deserves credit for opening up the area west of Lake Superior to trade in a peaceful environment.

The French recognized Duluth as being in charge of trading operations in the Lake Superior area and we know he continued his activities on and around the lake for several years. He established another post in 1684. This may have been the one at Nipigon.

De Noyon — 1687

This remarkable young man, barely out of his teens, was guided by local Indians through the Boundary Waters (probably the Kaministiquia route) to Rainy Lake, where he spent the winter. The next spring the Indians guided him to the Lake of the Woods which he named "Lake of the Isles". His explorations helped open the area west of Superior to trade.

Pierre Le Sueur — 1693

Le Sueur was given command of the Lake Superior area after Duluth. He constructed a post on Madeline Island in 1693. The next year he built a post at the mouth of the St. Croix. He spent a great deal of time on the Mississippi and its tributaries.[6]

Peace of Utrecht — 1713

This treaty between Great Britain and France had considerable impact on Lake Superior trade routes in that it gave Hudson's Bay to the British. The two countries had been fighting over that area since 1683. Hudson's Bay was the easiest access European nations had to the fur-rich North American wilderness. As a result of the treaty, France had to seek a new access to furs through the Great Lakes and water routes west of Lake Superior via Fond du Lac, Grand Portage and the Kaministiquia River.

De la Noue — 1717

There were probably other traders who followed De Noyon's route west of Superior before De la Noue, but we don't know who they were. We do know, however, that De la Noue re-established the trading post at the mouth of the Kaministiquia River (Thunder Bay) and that he later followed De Noyon's route to Rainy Lake, where he built another fort.

Pachot — 1722

Pachot is credited with making a map of the Grand Portage route to Rainy Lake. Because of easier portages and supposedly fewer insects, this then became the favored route for the traders and voyageurs until the early 1800s when it was discovered that this route was through United States territory and the Americans demanded duty be paid on goods in transit across U.S. soil. The English then moved their operations to Fort William and used the Kaministiquia route.

Pierre La Vérendrye — 1729

Here is a man who has never received adequate recognition for his contributions to exploration and to the development of the fur trade in mid-continent North America. He and his sons opened the area for trade from the Boundary Waters to the Red River and Lake Winnipeg. His explorations took him to the Dakotas and possibly as far as the foothills of the Rockies.

La Vérendrye was first named commander of a small fort on Lake Nipigon (or on Nipigon Bay[7]) in 1729 (possibly the one founded by Duluth in 1684). Here he learned from an Indian named "Auchgoh" about the Grand Portage route and about the Lake of the Woods. Auchgoh even drew a map for La Vérendrye on birchbark, copies of which are still in the French archives.

By 1731, La Vérendrye had organized an expedition of 49 men — out of Montreal, financed by the merchants of that city. At Mackinac he picked up a 50th member for his party, Father Measiger. It was customary for most French explorers to include a priest in their entourage.

The next stop was Kaministiquia (Fort William); in twelve weeks they had traveled a thousand miles. On August 6th they arrived at

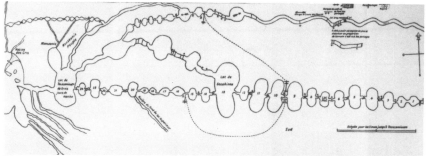

Tracing of a map drawn on birchbark by Auchagah and given to La Vérendrye. It shows both the Boundary Waters and Kaministiquia routes to Rainy Lake, Lake of the Woods, and points west. It has been preserved all these years in the French Archives.

Grand Portage, after traveling westward along the north shore of Lake Superior. "Grand Portage" meant a rugged nine mile climb up a rise of 650 feet from Lake Superior to the Pigeon River. Because of the lateness of the season and the rugged country ahead, most of the men opposed going further.[8] After serious deliberation, La Vérendrye agreed to return to Fort Kaministiquia on Lake Superior with the bulk of his crew. A smaller group — perhaps volunteers — agreed to go on under the leadership of a nephew, La Jemeraye. Jean Baptiste, the oldest son, accompanied the smaller group. This advanced contingent was able to reach Rainy Lake without incident and built a fort at the outlet of that lake before winter set in. It is believed that the structure was located on Pither's Point at the source of the Rainy River. The fort was named Fort St. Pierre, in honor of Pierre La Vérendrye.

In the spring of 1732, La Jemeraye returned to his uncle with a glowing report and canoes filled with furs. It is easy to imagine the ecstasy which must have filled the anxious heart of La Vérendrye after the long winter of waiting. Although the reunion at Grand Portage took place on May 29, the party did not arrive at Fort St. Pierre until July 14. A smaller party, meanwhile, had headed east after the reunion, bringing the canoes of furs back to Montreal to gladden the hearts of

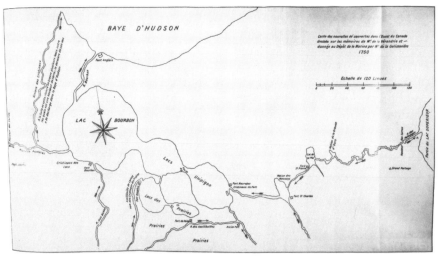

1750 map of Western Canada showing several of the La Vérendrye forts.

the merchant sponsors of the expedition. We are told that "a large gathering of Indians" met La Vérendrye upon his arrival at the Rainy River fort (St. Pierre). After considerable speechmaking and the exchanging of gifts, the adventurers, accompanied by about fifty Indian canoes, continued westward up the Rainy River to the Lake of the Woods. It must have been quite a spectacle.

After crossing Big Traverse, the party explored the inlets and islands of what is now the Northwest Angle, and finally selected a site on the mainland for the construction of the second fort. It was named "Fort St. Charles" — perhaps in honor of both the priest, Father Charles Measiger, and Charles de Beauharnois, the Governor of Canada. Many years later, after the fort had disappeared in decay, the dams at Kenora raised the level of Lake of the Woods, thus making the site of the fort an island (known today as Magnuson's Island).

In the spring of 1773, La Jemeraye (appointed second in command by his uncle) led a crew back east to report on the success of the mission. He took with him maps of their discoveries and furs collected over the winter. Father Measiger had been in ill health for some time and chose to return east with the party.

The years of 1733 and '34 were years of tension on the Lake of the Woods-Rainy Lake area. A raiding party of Dakota-Sioux had killed four Cree and this tribe and their allies were determined to gain revenge. La Vérendrye's efforts to maintain peace (so that he could continue his trading and exploring) succeeded only in delaying the action for a few months. In the spring of 1734 a small army of nearly 700 braves headed south to raid Sioux villages, probably on the Red Lakes. La Vérendrye's eldest son, Jean Baptiste, accompanied them; it was a price he had to pay in return for the Indians' promise to delay their revenge until spring. (La Vérendrye had hoped that by that time tempers would have cooled and plans for retaliation would have been abandoned).

This proved to be the prelude to all-out war between the Dakota-Sioux of Minnesota and the Ojibway-Assiniboine-Cree alliance of the border region and Wisconsin — a feud that was to last over 100 years, almost up to the time of the Civil War.

In 1736, a raiding party of the Dakota-Sioux of the prairies caught a party of La Vérendrye's men on their way to Mackinac to see why promised supplies had not arrived. The group was headed by his oldest son, Jean Baptiste, and included Father Alneau (who had replaced Father Mesaiger) and 19 soldier-voyageurs. All 21 were killed on a small island on the Lake of the Woods. The heads of the 19 crewmen and the headless bodies of the priest and young La Vérendrye were buried in the chapel back at Fort St. Charles. The discovery of these remains in 1908 verified the location of the fort.[9]

Pierre La Vérendrye and his sons led many expeditions back and forth across Lake Superior between Montreal and the western forts.

Other Significant French Traders of the 1700s

Bourassa, a contemporary of La Vérendrye's and mentioned in his journals, is credited with building a fort at the mouth of the Vermillion River on or near Crane Lake.

Nicolas Joseph de Noyelles, Jackques de **St. Pierre** and Louis Francois de **la Corne** were all commandants at Fort Charles in the years after the La Vérendryes. They and the voyageurs who serviced the fort used the trade routes across Lake Superior.

The Indian Wars, Tribe Against Tribe

Following the Lake of the Woods massacre in 1736, war broke out between the Dakota-Sioux and Algonquin tribes. La Vérendrye and other Frenchmen insisted they wanted no revenge and tried to keep the peace. When it became apparent that the Crees, Monsonis[10] and incoming Ojibway were going to attack the Sioux, the Frenchmen reminded them that the Dakota-Sioux of the woodlands were not involved in the raid — rather it was the Sioux of the plains. But they paid no heed. In fact, the Ojibway from La Pointe (Madeline Island on Lake Superior) attacked the Sioux as far south as Lake Pepin.)

In three short years following the Lake of the Woods massacre, the Dakotas were dislodged from all of their northern Minnesota strongholds.

The first attacks on the northern Sioux villages were not by the Ojibway, but by their allies the Crees and Assiniboins from the north. Launching their attack from their Lake of the Woods and boundary water villages, they drove down on the Red Lakes, Winnibigoshish, Cass, and then Leech. The Ojibway seemed almost reluctant at first to join the battle. Perhaps it was because their leadership still felt a loyalty to the French and their pursuit of peace among the tribes. However, when they had once committed themselves, it was with a vengeance. The Dakota villages at Sandy Lake fell to the Ojibway — and this site was to become the new capital of the Ojibway Nation. Located on the watershed between Lake Superior and the Mississippi lake region at the end of the Savanna portage, it was the key to control of the entire area.

By 1739, the Dakotas had fled from their lake area strongholds and had moved their families to the prairies, and back into the southern part of the state, particularly along the Minnesota River. The once powerful Mille Lacs village of Kathio—what was left of it—was moved to the mouth of the Rum River. But the war was by no means over. It was really the beginning of a hundred years' war. No sooner would the Sioux be driven from an area than they would plan a counterattack. If the Ojibway or their allies moved out of an area, the Dakotas moved back in. Sometimes old village sites were even resettled by the original Sioux families. Although the Dakotas had been driven from their strongholds, they certainly had not given up; nor were the Ojibway and their allies strong enough to occupy and control the area. When villages were first established by the Ojibway and their allies, they were often wiped out — women, children and all. All of northern Minnesota soon became a virtual "no man's land" inhabited mostly by marauding war parties. The bands were not large — usually less than 100 braves in number. From 1739 to 1766, few tried to "live" in the area, and all who entered did so with intent to wage war. But when the ice went out of the lakes in the spring of 1766, the Ojibway organized an army of about 400 warriors from their villages along Lake Superior and throughout Wisconsin. When the war party left Fond du Lac it was said that a man standing on a high hill could not see the end or the beginning of the line formed by the Indians walking in single file — as was their custom.

By mid-May, the better-armed Ojibways had met and soundly

defeated a much larger "army" of Dakotas, perhaps as many as 600 braves. The Dakotas at first fell back to Leech Lake and solidified their forces. Their first strategy was to occupy the islands of the lake. If they had been content to wait it out here until reinforcements arrived, they would have been relatively safe and could have held out for some time. However, over eager and over confident, the Dakotas made a grave error in strategy. They divided their forces and launched three simultaneous attacks on Pembina, Rainy Lake and Sandy Lake. They lost on all three fronts and the resultant disaster was the turning point of the war. The Sioux fell back to their villages west of the Mississippi and along the Minnesota River. The Dakota stronghold remained at the mouth of the Rum River.

The Ojibway were, for the first time, truly in control of the lake region and a serious effort was made to settle the area. Sandy Lake continued as the headquarters for their operations but villages soon appeared on the Red Lakes, Winnibigoshish, Cass Lake, Leech Lake and Mille Lacs. Just as the islands of Leech Lake had been the last strongholds of the Dakotas they became the first homes of the Ojibway in the area. For even though the Ojibway had effectively defeated the Dakotas, Sioux war parties would return again and again for many years to view their old village sites, visit the burial places of their ancestors, and administer vengeance to the Ojibways. In fact, if the Ojibway villages had not been replenished continuously with settlers from the east, they surely would have been annihilated.

The fighting among the tribes continued, sporadically, almost up to the time of the Civil War.[11] But after 1770, the fighting subsided sufficiently for the Lake Superior trade routes to once again be busy with voyageur canoes.

Effects of the Treaty of Paris — 1763 ← *The Northwest Territory*

Although the French were the first white men in the border country and pretty much dominated the area for a hundred years or more, their influence was to be brought to an end by wars fought on distant battle fields (both on and off this continent) where the French and their Indian allies lost to the British (French and Indian War). The treaty ending the war, and signed in Paris in 1763, gave this part of North America to the English. There had been a diminishing of French activity along the border waterways prior to this time because of the Indian wars and a few British traders took advantage of the void, even prior to the signing of the treaty. But they too left and, so far as we know, there were no whites west of Lake Superior just after 1763. The few who tried to enter were plundered and rebuffed by the Indians.

By the time trading resumed after 1770 following the Indian wars, the British were in control of the major trading operations, including both the south and north shores of Lake Superior and the fur-rich area west of the lake.

The Fur Trade Company Rivalries

By 1770, with the Sioux pushed into what is now southern Minnesota and west to the Dakotas and with the Ojibway settled into the village sites in the woodlands and with the friendly Cree and Assiniboine to the north, trade once again picked up.

The Hudson's Bay Company had a presence in what is now northern Canada for 100 years prior to this time and for the most part had been successful in persuading the Indians to travel north to Hudson's Bay or at least north of Lake Winnipeg to exchange their furs for trade goods. This was surely easier access for Europeans than crossing half the continent. But with the coming of the La Vérendryes in the 1730s, the company began to feel the competition and in the 1770s, following the Indian wars, began establishing posts to the south. By 1793 they had established a trading post on Rainy River at Manitou Falls.

As the Hudson's Bay Company moved south, the independent traders formed the North West Company to compete. For a time a splinter group spun off from the North West Company; they called themselves "the XY Company". In the face of the expanding and powerful Hudson's Bay Company, however, the two groups agreed to reunite in 1815. Even so, the North West Company was never more than a loose confederation of traders and trading companies, making it difficult to compete against the better organized Hudson's Bay Company.

The conflict between the two major companies became intense. At first the hostilities were limited to the men from the different companies making it difficult for each other to do their work and each company trying various techniques to entice the Indians to trade with them — such as using rum as a trade item or giving the Indians trade goods before they harvested the furs. But by the early 1800s there was violence and even bloodshed.

Lord Selkirk of the H.B.C. had established a fledgling colony[12] near present day Winnipeg and St. Boniface with intentions of settling a much larger area. He called his new country "Assiniboia". The North West Company saw this as a grave threat and with the help of Indians attacked the colony, killing more than 20 including the governor,[13] and took others as prisoners.

Lord Selkirk retaliated (1816) by hiring Swiss mercenaries fresh from the Napoleonic wars and captured the North West forts from Fort William on Lake Superior all the way west to Fort Douglas where the Assiniboine and Red Rivers meet.

Because of this show of strength by the Hudson's Bay Company and because everyone was losing as the competition turned bloody, the two companies finally merged in 1821. Sir George Simpson of the HBC was the chief architect of the merger. It is interesting that inspite of all the earlier hostility, the merger provided for some of the officers of the North West Company — even those who had opposed the merger such as Dr. McLaughlin — to assume roles of leadership in the merged company. In other words, it was a true merger, not a take-over.

The North West posts on Lake Superior were all renamed as Hudson's Bay operations.

War of 1812

In the middle of the trade war, there was another war going on between Great Britain and her former colony, the United States. As we know, the war of 1812 settled little. The young United States did remain free but lost most major battles and even suffered the humiliation of having its Capitol and White House burned in Washington D.C. British forces in the Lake Superior area had no trouble taking charge. Lt. Thomas Bennett occupied Grand Portage and other British loyalists occupied other posts as far south as Lake Pepin, as well as all around Lake Superior. The British gave commissions to the traders in the Lake Superior region and directed them to recruit Indians to fight the Americans. The Dakota-Sioux, largely through the efforts of Leech Lake trader Col. Robert Dickson, joined forces with the English. The Ojibway, however, stayed neutral through the leadership of such men as Chief Flat Mouth[14] of Leech Lake. Because the Ojibway announced they would not join the British, the Sioux were afraid to leave their villages unprotected, thus thwarting the hopes of the British to mount an offensive against the United States from the west with the help of an army of Indian warriors.

After the war, the British gradually withdrew across the border.

Defining a Border[15]

The Minnesota-Ontario border was established by a treaty signed in Paris in 1783, ending the American Revolutionary War, but it took until 1925 to establish final agreement on the last segment of the border at the Northwest Angle of the Lake of the Woods. During the intervening years, the boundary was defined almost lake by lake and portage by portage. This was done by the Joint Boundary Commission (U.S. and British) that agreed on the line as instructed by the Treaty of Ghent (1814) after the War of 1812. Lewis Cass is given credit for raising the first U.S. flag on Lake Superior in 1820.

The United States realized that Grand Portage was on American soil and in 1800 announced that British trade goods carried on that route would have to pay duty. The English were not anxious to use the more difficult Fort William-Kaministiquia River route to Rainy Lake but by 1803, having little choice, moved their operations to Fort William. It was also in 1803 that the United States purchased the huge territory of Louisiana (almost everything west of the Mississippi River) from Napoleon. In 1805, Lt. Zebulon Pike[16] was sent up the Mississippi to advise the North West Company posts as far north as Sandy and Leech Lakes (part of the Fond du Lac Department) that they would have to operate under the rules and regulations of the United States government.

Once the boundary was more clearly defined, the American Fur Company, founded in 1808 by John Jacob Astor, began taking over trading operations on the U.S. side of the border. In 1817, they bought out the North West Company operations out of Fond du Lac (serving what is now Minnesota and part of Wisconsin). By 1823, 40 years after the signing of the treaty ending the Revolutionary War, the transition was complete and traders stayed on their own sides of the border.

All of this, of course, had implications for traffic on Lake Superior.

Other Early Explorers and Traders on Lake Superior

John Askin

in 1766 cleared ground for the construction of the huge North West fort at Grand Portage.

Jonathan Carver

visited Grand Portage on his way home from what is now called Minnesota in 1767. He had hoped to find traders there so that he could replenish his supplies and continue his explorations. He found none in residence but he did find "300 friendly Indians". He finally joined some voyageurs returning from the west via the Boundary Waters and traveled with them across Lake Superior and to Montreal. He was on the lake again in 1776 and reported that the French were using a small schooner to carry trade goods and furs across the lake.

Peter Pond

is credited with discovering the Methye Portage which opened Athabasca to traders and voyageurs and this significantly increased the flow of trade across Lake Superior.

Alexander Henry, the elder

was the first Englishman licensed to trade on Lake Superior and the area to the west after the British acquired the territory through the French and Indian War. He and a man named Baker were authorized to mine copper. (They also found silver.) He was headquartered at Madeline Island as early as 1765.

Perrault

was an early visitor to the Duluth-Superior area. He reported finding a trader, **Du fault,** on Rice's Point (Duluth) in 1784. Perrault then traveled via the St. Louis River and the Savanna Portage to Sandy Lake and Pine River. He and six other traders returned to Fond du Lac in 1789. They cooperated with each other and built trading houses on Leech, Red and Ottertail Lakes and on Pine River. All of the furs were funneled through Fond du Lac.

In 1793, Perrault was directed by the North West Company to construct a permanent fort at Fond du Lac. He chose Conner's Point (Superior) and named it "Fort St. Louis".

Alexander Henry, the younger
continued to develop trade west of Lake Superior in the early 1800s.

Sir Alexander Mackenzie, the elder
was a partner in the North West Company — in charge of Fort Chipewyan on Lake Athabasca — the western terminal point for many voyageurs. From here he made an expedition to the Arctic Ocean in 1789, for which achievement the Mackenzie River was given his name. In 1793 this remarkable man pressed across the plains, through the wilderness and over the mountains to the Pacific, thus becoming the first white man to cross the continent north of Mexico! He then returned to England where he wrote his *Voyages* and was knighted. He came back to Canada in 1802 and became the leading partner in the XY Company. After 1804, when the North West Company and the XY Company were reunited, Mackenzie once more became a partner in the North West Company.

Alexander Mackenzie, the younger
was a nephew of Sir Alexander and worked under him in the XY Company. After the merger with the North West Company, he also became a partner in the united company. Most of his work was at the posts along the shores of Lake Superior, but he also served at the fort on Lake Athabasca and was in the boundary waters on several occasions. Lord Selkirk had him arrested as a contributor to the Seven Oaks Massacre, but he was acquitted in a trial at York.

John Jacob Astor
founded the American Fur Company in 1808 and made it a viable competitor to the Hudson's Bay Company and the North West Company. After the U.S.-Canadian border was roughly established in this region in 1821, he monopolized the fur trade south of the border, including the south shore and the U.S. portion of the North Shore. Most of his operations on Lake Superior itself, however, involved commercial fishing. His company began operations at Fond du Lac in 1809. The British moved them out during the War of 1812, but they returned after the war and, as we have already mentioned, Astor bought out the remaining North West Company operations in the Fond du Lac Department in 1817.

Henry Schoolcraft

was particularly influential on the lake in the 1820s and the 1830s. He is best known today for his discovery of the source of the Mississippi River — Lake Itasca. He spent most of his time, however, on Lake Superior. He served as Indian Agent at Sault Ste. Marie and his domain was Lake Superior and everything west — including present day Michigan, Wisconsin and Minnesota. Fond du Lac and Grand Portage were both in his jurisdiction. He was really enchanted with Lake Superior, pointing out that it was more like a sea or even an ocean. After all, he noted, it is so large it does generate its own weather systems. He was also devoted to the Algonquin tribes and suggested changing the name of the lake to "Algona — the Sea of the Algonquins".

David Thompson

was among the important English explorers who traversed Lake Superior. Born in London, England, he attended Oxford before coming to this continent around 1784. He was at first apprenticed to the Hudson's Bay Company, but went to work for the rival North West Company in 1797. Thompson spent many years in the border country, making a significant contribution as a map maker, basing his work on his knowledge of astronomy and the readings he took establishing latitudes and longitudes. His work carried him to the far west where he discovered the Columbia River in 1807. He returned to Canoe Country when he was placed in charge of the British Commission to develop the United States-Canada boundary from the St. Lawrence River to the Lake of the Woods. He also ventured deeper into Minnesota where he erroneously proclaimed Turtle Lake (near Bemidji) as the source of the Mississippi River. Thompson was a pretty fair artist and provided the illustrations for Bigsby's *The Shoe and Canoe*, which gave the world its first view of the B.W.C.A.

Dr. John Bigsby

served with Thompson as a member of the British Commission to establish the U.S.-Canadian border. Bigsby Island on Lake of the Woods bears his name. As assistant secretary to the Commission, he kept and published a diary entitled, *The Shoe and Canoe*.

Major Joseph Delafield

was in charge of the American portion of the Joint Boundary Commission established to identify the U.S.-Canadian border as provided in The Treaty of Ghent (1814). His journals were published under the title *The Unfortified Boundary*.

Sir George Simpson

was a partner in the operations of the Hudson's Bay Company. The H. B. C. operations on Rainy Lake had always been known as the "Lac la Pluie" post, but the name was changed to "Fort Frances" in honor of

Mrs. Simpson when she visited there with her husband in 1830 as a bride of but a few months. Sir George was influential in bringing about the merger of the Hudson's Bay Company and the North West Company in 1821. He was appointed governor of the northern part of the united company and later served as the general superintendent. Simpson encouraged exploration and he, himself, crossed the continent and made a trip around the world in 1841-'42. Sir George liked to travel in style and his canoe was usually propelled by a select group of voyageurs — making his craft the fastest in the north country. A bagpipe playing musician usually accompanied him. One wonders what the wolves, loons and other members of the wild kingdom thought when they heard the unique tones of this remarkable instrument, and how they may have responded! It is said that he crossed Lake Superior 100 times and knew it as well as any man.

Dr. John McLaughlin

The Canadian-born physician-explorer spent several years in the area sometimes wintering at Little Vermilion Lake. In 1814 he was made a partner in the North West Company and was placed in charge of the Rainy River District. While at the Rainy Lake post, he successfully treated John Tanner,[17] who had been ambushed and nearly killed on his way east. As the only physician in the area he no doubt had ample opportunity to ply his trade. He was also stationed at the Grand Portage post for a time.

Dr. John McLoughlin
Courtesy Public Archives of Canada

McLaughlin opposed the union with the Hudson's Bay Company, but after the merger, accepted a commission as chief factor. In 1823 he was placed in charge of the Columbia Department on the west coast. Because of his work and leadership in that area he is known to this day as "the Father of Oregon". In 1824 he took charge of Fort George (Astoria); in 1826 he moved farther north where he constructed Fort Vancouver. In his later years, McLaughlin left the Hudson's Bay Company and started a general store in Oregon City, and there lived out his legendary life.

Lord Thomas Selkirk

Lake Superior was the gateway to the establishment of an experimental colony in the wilderness of North America, a true story as spectacular as fiction. The colony was the dream of British-born Lord Thomas Selkirk, a dream inspired by letters from the brother of an assistant, Miles Macdonell. The brother, John Macdonell, had passed through the border area as early as 1793, on his way to the prairies of Saskatchewan, and had kept a diary of his experiences. Selkirk wanted to help the disadvantaged of his day and envisioned the American colony as the vehicle.

Lord Selkirk

To make his dream a reality, the English nobleman believed he needed a great deal of land, and since the Hudson's Bay Company was the chief landholder in the area in which he was interested, he engineered the purchase of a controlling share of Hudson's Bay Company stock (at a time when the company was in financial difficulty because of the naval blockades during the Napoleonic wars). The North West Company was well aware of Selkirk's plans and strongly opposed them — first through an unsuccessful effort by Sir Alexander Mackenzie to get control of a large block of Hudson's Bay stock, and later by violence and bloodshed. Meanwhile, Selkirk used his position to arrange the cession to himself of 116,000 square miles of territory, including Rainy Lake, much of the Rainy River basin, Lake of the Woods, and stretching as far west as the Red River of the North. He called his new land "Assiniboia", after the tribe of Sioux Indians living in the area. Settlers soon arrived from the British Isles (and later from Switzerland) and developed a colony near the present site of Winnipeg and St. Boniface, Manitoba. The North West Company answered with a show of force, capturing the Hudson's Bay's posts in the area and destroying the embryonic villages along the Red River, killing twenty or more of the colonists — including the man Selkirk had made governor, John Semple — and taking others prisoner. It became known as the "Seven Oaks Massacre".

Selkirk struck back by hiring mercenaries from the Napoleonic wars — mostly Swiss. He placed a man named Peter Fidler in charge of capturing the first target, the Rainy Lake Post, in the winter of 1816. However, when the North West Company clerk, J.W. Dease, was called on to surrender, he calmly refused. Fidler was not certain he had enough men to storm the fort, so he returned all the way to Fort William for reinforcements and a pair of small cannons. This time, badly outnumbered, Dease gave up the Rainy Lake Post without a fight. Now Selkirk's men were ready to proceed west to attack the Red River forts. Being winter, they felt the need for a guide to show them the shorter routes across land, so they hired John Tanner — the "white

Indian", the "Falcon" from Lake of the Woods — along with about twenty of his braves. Selkirk had placed a Captain D'Orsonnens in charge of this expedition and his aide, Mike Macdonell, also joined the group.

According to Tanner, he chose the traditional Indian route, via the Roseau bogs and river. Fort Daer (at Pembina) gave up without a fight, but Fort Douglas (where the Red and Assiniboine Rivers meet) was no such easy mark. While the mercenaries were bickering over the best way to attack, Tanner and his men, augmented by a few of the more venturesome Swiss soldiers, scaled the stockade at night, surprised the defenders and captured the fort. In appreciation, Lord Selkirk took a deep, personal interest in Tanner and rewarded him with a twenty pound per year stipend for life.

The H.B.C. forces captured all significant North West Company posts including Fort William and Fort St. Louis on Lake Superior.

Selkirk was now free to restore his colonies, and he did. These communities eventually developed strong ties with St. Paul and Minneapolis via the Red River ox cart trails. In fact, about 300 of the Swiss settlers grew disillusioned and followed the trails one way — to Fort Snelling (in the 1820s), carrying their possessions in ox carts and driving their livestock before them. But many remained in Selkirk's colonies and with the coming of first the Dawson Trail, and then the railroad, ties were established with eastern Canada — and the metropolis of Winnipeg was born — something far beyond even the imaginative dreams of Lord Thomas Selkirk.

Peter Grant
was a partner in charge, for a time, of the Rainy River District of the North West Company. He followed Boyer and Shoults as commander of the Rainy Lake post and spent at least one winter (1805) at the fort on Little Vermilion Lake, thus indicating by his presence (as a partner) that it was indeed important to the operations of the company.

John Cameron
son of a loyalist who fled to Canada during the American Revolution, at first served with the North West Company and was appointed chief factor of the Columbia District under the merger. In 1824 he exchanged positions with Dr. McLaughlin and remained in charge of the Rainy Lake District until 1832.

Major Stephen Long
represented the United States in determining the location of the 49th parallel in 1823 the boundary between Canada and the United States west of the Lake of the Woods as specified in the Convention of 1818 which followed the War of 1812.

William McGillivray

was a partner in the North West Company and commandant during the peak of activity at the post at the mouth of the Kaministiquia River at Thunder Bay. The huge fort, including a stockade and a number of buildings, was built in 1803 as the British were forced to phase out their operations on U.S. soil at Grand Portage. It was known as Fort Kaministiquia until 1805 when it was renamed Fort William to honor McGillivray who by then was superintendent of the company.

Simon McGillivray

son of William McGillivray for whom Fort William was named, authored the 1825 Hudson Bay Co. report for the Rainy Lake District. His mother was an Ojibway. McGillivray was privileged to travel in Europe and was highly respected by the leadership of the fur industry of that day.

Roderick McKenzie

succeeded Robert Logan as commander of the Rainy Lake post. In the records of the 1819-1820 season, he told of the first mass migration of settlers through the boundary waters, bound for the Red River colonies. They followed the Fort William Kaministiquia River route to Lac La Croix, where it joined the traditional route which originated at Grand Portage and the Pigeon River.

Simon Dawson and Henry Hind

In 1857, the Canadian government assigned Dawson, a surveyor-explorer, and Hind, a naturalist, the task of finding the elusive all-Canadian route to the Red River colonies. They searched in vain for the old Indian trail via the Warroad River, Hay Creek and Roseau River — with portages in between. On Lake of the Woods they were surprised to find the Indians engaged in quite a farming operation on Garden Island with several acres under cultivation. When the Indians caught them sampling their crops they scolded them and refused to show them their secret route to the Red River country. Actually, it wouldn't have been of much help anyway because it crossed United States soil.

Although they failed in their primary mission, Hind learned and recorded a great deal about the plant and animal life of the area.

Dr. George M. Dawson

was commissioned in 1873 to find an all-Canadian route from Montreal to the Red River and Lake Winnipeg to service the fledgling colonies founded by Lord Selkirk.

In his first effort he discovered the Roseau River route from Lake of the Woods west—the same as used by Tanner in leading Selkirk's Swiss mercenaries in their recapture of Forts Daer and Douglas. This proved unsatisfactory because it crossed American soil.

The ultimate solution was to use the established waterways from Lake Superior to Lake of the Woods, portages and all, and then carve a road through the wilderness west of the lake to the prairies. Thus, the "Dawson Trail" became a reality, starting where Harrison's Creek flows into the Angle Inlet and ending at Fort Garry (Winnipeg). The route from the Angle west was all by land, first by ox carts and later by stage lines. By 1874, the Dominion Government had spent a million and a quarter dollars (no mean sum for those days) on the Dawson route, and in that year more than 300 emigrants followed it to the Red River and Lake Winnipeg area.

The Dominion Government was so determined to break through the wilderness that even a proposal to develop a system of canals from Lake Superior to Lake of the Woods was taken very seriously. At one point the administration proceeded with the actual construction of a canal at Fort Frances and a large number of men were moved into the area. These became the first permanent settlers in the Fort Frances-International Falls region and along the south shore of Lake of the Woods. However, a change in administration in 1875 resulted in the plan being postponed and then dropped altogether.

Missionaries

It was the custom of the early explorers to include a "man of God" in their party. La Vérendrye had Father Mesaiger and, later, Father Alneau; Joliet had Father Marquette; La Salle had Father Hennepin; Schoolcraft had Rev. Boutwell, and so on.

Many of these missionaries did some exploring on their own and because they were often better educated than their sponsors, had more impact through their writings than did the explorers themselves. But their primary role was to convert the Native Americans to Christianity — and this effort met with varying degrees of success.

In many cases they endured severe hardships and sometimes became discouraged. Listen to Father Alneau in his report to his superiors from Fort Charles on the Lake of the Woods:

"As for the Indians who dwell here, I do not believe, unless it is by a miracle, that they can ever be persuaded to embrace the faith; for even not taking into account the fact that they have no fixed abode, and that they wander about the forests in isolated bands, they are superstitious and morally degraded to a degree beyond conception. In addition both the English and the French, by their accursed avarice, have given them a taste for brandy and this traffic in liquor with the Indians has brought about the destruction of several flourishing missions, and has induced many an Indian to cast away every semblance of religion. This practice constitutes one of the greatest crosses the missionaries have to endure here among the Indians."

Alneau, of course, became the first martyr in the western wilderness. An article on the Oberlin band of missionaries by William

Bigglestone in the Spring 1976 Issue of *Minnesota History* gives us great insight into hardships endured by the early missionaries — and others — while traveling across the wilderness. Bigglestone quotes the *Oberlin Evangelist* of May 10, 1843, as follows:

"It was deep into the winter of 1842-43 when three men slowly worked their way through the frozen swamps and forests to the west and northwest of Lake Superior. They followed Indian trails and each evening at sundown stopped to make camp. Logs 8 to 10 feet in length were cut to feed an all-night fire, and balsam fir branches were gathered for the foundation of a bed. After the snow had been cleared away with a snowshoe there was room for a fire, a bed, two dogs and the loaded sled that the dogs pulled. When twigs or dry grass had been laid atop the branches of the bed, the three put on dry leggings and moccasins, ate supper, sang a hymn, and united in prayer. They then lay down together on the one bed, sometimes wearing caps, coats, and mittens because they had not room to carry sufficient bedding for the extreme cold. If the wind blew too fiercely they put up a row of branches to break its force and hoped the fire would not have to be renewed often during the night. They arose before daylight for a breakfast of rice or boiled corn meal thickened with flour and sweetened by a little sugar, and, while preparing it, they also baked bread cakes which served as a noon meal that could be eaten while walking."

The three men described were Frederick Ayer, David Spencer and a young Ojibway guide named Yellow Bird; their destination was Red Lake. Bigglestone also tells of a summer journey from Oberlin College to Red Lake by a party headed by S.T. Bardwell and which included three men, three women and some children:

"Among the obstacles they faced were cholera and other illness; flooding rivers; mosquitoes so thick they were almost inhaled when one drew breath; straying horses; portages with mud and water higher than boot tops; flies so thick their bites left a child's hair matted in her blood under her bonnet and her ear filled with clotted blood; high winds that almost swamped canoes as the crossed lakes; and summer heat that rose to a temperature of a hundred degrees."

The following are additional clergymen who were associated with the Lake Superior region:

Fathers Joques and Ramibault

visited the rapids between Lakes Huron and Superior in 1641 and named them Sault Ste. Marie in honor of the Virgin Mary. It is interesting that Lake Superior was explored before Lakes Michigan, Erie and Ontario. The French were afraid of the hostile Iroquois.

Father Allouez

built the first permanent mission at Sault Ste. Marie in 1665.

Father Marquette

traveled extensively with Joillet and they are credited with being the first whites to travel on the Upper Mississippi River. He built the first cabin on what now is the American side of Sault Ste. Marie in 1668.

Father Pierz

was an historic figure in the settling and development of central and northern Minnesota. He was born in Austria and recruited many immigrants from central Europe. He is also remembered for negotiating peace with Chief Hole-in-the-Day at Gull Lake.[18] He established schools and missions as far north as the Red Lakes and at Grand Portage (1838). He was also at Fond du Lac.

Father Baraga

a contemporary of Father Pierz and also from Austria, was headquartered at La Pointe at the church of St. Joseph. He was allowed to travel at will on boats operated by the American Fur Company.

In 1846, after enduring a hazardous and stormy crossing of the lake in a canoe (from La Pointe) he came ashore at a stream now known as "Cross River". In gratitude for his safe arrival, he erected a wooden cross at the mouth of the stream.

Rev. Boutwell

a Presbyterian, traveled with Henry Schoolcraft and suggested "Itasca" as the name for the source of the Mississippi. It is taken from two Latin words meaning "true head". Boutwell serviced the posts in the Fond du Lac Department, spending more time on Leech Lake than anywhere else. He was probably the first Protestant minister to preach at Fond du Lac and he was married there.

Rev. Ely

a colleague of Boutwell, serviced the Protestant (Presbyterian) mission at Fond du Lac and Sandy Lake. From 1834 into the 1850s he was instrumental in platting and recording properties from Fond du Lac west even before white settlers were allowed to claim property (1854).

There are other explorers, traders and missionaries whose names are known but whose impact on Lake Superior was not deemed important enough by the author to receive special mention in this book. There have no doubt been some errors in judgment and for that we willingly apologize. No doubt there were also hundreds more, some who traveled with the well-known explorers, whose exploits were significant to the lake but whose names are not known, and that is regrettable. They were heroes too, and they left their mark on Lake Superior and Lake Superior, no doubt, left its mark on them.

[1]The Minnesota Historical Society officially doubts the authenticity of the Runestone.

[2]For further information on La Vérendrye's visit to the Mandans, consult *Lake of the Woods Volume II, Earliest Accounts*, by this author.

[3]Groseilliers, the older of the two, eventually left the company and associated himself with his fellow countrymen — the French, but Radisson married an English woman and stayed with the company, dying in England in 1710 at the age of 74.

[4]For more information about the dramatic execution of La Pointe by the Ojibway, consult *Tales of Four Lakes and a River* by this author.

[5]For further information on Duluth's travels in Minnesota, consult *Tales of Four Lakes and a River* by this author.

[6]For further information on LeSueur's expeditions on the Mississippi, consult *Our Historical Upper Mississippi* by this author.

[7]We know there was a large fort at the head of Nipigon Bay still operating in 1775.

[8]Their opposition bordered on mutiny.

[9]For further information about the La Vérendryes, consult *Lake of the Woods, Yesterday and Today*, and *Lake of the Woods, Volume II*, both by this author.

[10]Algonquin — Ojibway related.

[11]For more information about the tribal wars, consult *Our Historic Upper Mississippi* by this author.

[12]For more information concerning Lord Selkirk's colony, consult *Tales of Four Lakes and a River* and *Our Historic Upper Mississippi* by this author.

[13]A Leech Lake Ojibway, named Maji-gabo, took "credit" for the slaying and scalping of Governor Semple. Schoolcraft once met and described Maji-gabo as "tall, gaunt, and savage looking."

[14]For more information about this great chief, consult *Tales of Four Lakes* by this author.

[15]For more detailed information about resolving the border, consult *Our Historic Boundary Waters* by this author, and *Lake of the Woods, Volume I*.

[16]For more information about the Pike expedition, consult *Our Historic Upper Mississippi* by this author.

[17]The "Falcon" — white Indian of Lake of the Woods fame. For further information, consult *White Indian Boy* by this author — the story of John Tanner.

[18]For more information on the narrowly averted Ojibway uprising, consult *Tales of Four Lakes and a River* by this author.

CHAPTER III
THE VOYAGEURS

So great their achievements, so spectacular their endurance, so colorful their attire, so unique their mission — they could have come out of fiction or modern day adventure comics — but they were very much for real — these voyageurs of our North American wilderness.

In the history of man there has never been a system of trade or transportation quite like it. Few physical accomplishments can match those achieved by the voyageurs; they demanded as much of their bodies as Olympic athletes — and it was no one time venture — it was repeated again and again for more than two hundred years!

When, where and how did it all begin? It started in the 1600s with the French settlements along the St. Lawrence River. As we have already stated, a demand was created in Europe for American furs almost as soon as the colonies became a reality. Man had worn the skins of animals from the beginning, but during the days of the great European empires, furs really came into their own with their practical, durable beauty. Earlier in history they had been reserved in some countries for royalty only; this, of course, added to their prestige and desirability. With the discovery of a seemingly endless supply in North America, the demand for furs simply exploded. Furthermore, the American fur-bearing animals were generally larger than their European cousins. The Indians added an exotic touch by wearing furs next to their bodies in winter. These hides went for a premium because the body oils gave the fur a special sheen and body friction softened the pelts.

The St. Lawrence valley was once rich in furs, especially that of the coveted beaver, but the supply was quickly depleted by heavy trapping. In order to bring in even more hides from the remote regions, trade fairs were held in places like Quebec and Montreal. However, the fur business became so lucrative some of the more enterprising traders intercepted the Indians on their way east and did their trading out in the wilderness, thus drying up the source of furs for the trade

The dress was as colorful as the voyageurs themselves.

fairs. Competition soon forced exploration of the Great Lakes and the streams that emptied into those great bodies of water and, before long, forts and their auxiliary trading posts were under construction. The French government felt the need to regulate the fur industry and began licensing the traders. As the traders ventured west they needed help, so they engaged men from the villages along the St. Lawrence River to paddle the canoes and do the many chores; these men were at first called "engagees". Later they were more appropriately called "voyageurs", which in French simply means "travelers".

It wasn't long before posts were established all along the shores of the Great Lakes. We saw in the last chapter how Duluth developed an operation on the North Shore of Lake Superior in 1679. Soon thereafter men like De Noyon penetrated the Boundary Waters and reached the Lake of the Woods in 1688 or '89. But it was a Yankee, Peter Pond, who was guided by the Indians across the 12-mile Methye Portage to Clearwater River and Lake Athabasca in 1787, thus making it possible (more than one hundred years after the first voyageurs hit the trail) to harvest furs in the area we now call "Saskatchewan" nearly 3,000 miles west of Montreal.

Meanwhile, the voyageurs became an institution with fairly uniform traditions, techniques, skills and even food and dress. They were also alike in size and general physical appearance. Although strength and endurance were important attributes for the voyageur, size was actually a handicap. There just wasn't room in the canoes for big men — the more human weight the less room for the payload. Thus most voyageurs were about five and a half feet tall, or less, and usually of slight build, but wiry.

Those who knew them firsthand have recorded that voyageurs were also much alike in character and disposition. We are told they were volatile in emotion, fiercely proud of their occupation, eager to meet a physical challenge, loyal, honest, meticulously polite and basically religious. Their vices (or they would say, "pleasures") were smoking, drinking and occasional gambling. We are led to believe that nearly every voyageur carried a clay pipe and tobacco pouch on his sash. On the more difficult portages or on long stretches of water he was given a smoking break each hour ("poses") — and we read that the cloud of smoke that hung over the portages long after the men had passed on their way was testimony to the enthusiasm with which they enjoyed their repass. In fact, distance was measured in "poses" or by "the pipe" rather than in miles. Drinking, on the other hand, was more carefully regulated by those in charge — and was saved for special occasions or as rewards. High wine was apparently the most common strong drink.

Their dress was as colorful as the voyageurs themselves. In the early years they were clothed much like their Indian friends (from whom they learned so much): moccasins, buckskin leggings, a breechcloth and bare skin from the waist up. In colder weather they would wear a deerskin jacket of sorts. In later years, the more practical cloth garments became more common. A blue or red hooded jacket seemed to be a favorite, and nearly everyone wore a gaily colored sash. Neck scarves were also common and a cap of some kind was universal. Most were made of wool and red was the favorite color — with a tassel — usually dropping alongside the ear. When their hair grew too long, they might braid it. Sometimes a feather was added to the cap as a special touch; imported ostrich plumes were preferred to those of native birds.

The voyageurs are as well remembered for their singing as for their dress. Never have men sung more lustily at their work. It must have been a very special experience to hear the songs of the voyageurs drifting across the waters through the early morning fog. Most of the chansons were timed to synchronize their brisk paddling; all were designed to lift their spirits — even those that were about long lost sweethearts and home. Many of the songs had crossed the Atlantic with the French immigrants; others were composed along the St. Lawrence; and still others were spontaneous and original. Many have been preserved to this day — every boy scout knows the swinging melody of "Alouette". A few of the songs were even religious, reminding the voyageurs while carrying canoes or packs along the portage, for example, of Christ carrying his cross. Singing was so important to morale and performance, that a good lead-singer was often given extra pay.

The voyageurs got along well with the Indians and they accepted them as equals. They befriended them, intermarried with them, and counted the braves as brothers. The English, in contrast, generally kept the Indians at arm's length and at best developed a paternalistic attitude towards them.

Each spring as the ice went out, the voyageurs left Montreal and headed west. By tradition, each man stopped at St. Anne's church (their patron saint) to make a contribution to the collection box for the work of the church and to seek a blessing and assure a safe return. The canoes fought the current up the Ottawa River, then the Mattawa to Trout Lake. After a portage into Nipissing, it was "downhill" on the French River to Lake Huron, past Sault Ste. Marie, into Lake Superior, and then west across our great inland sea arriving at Grand Portage (or Fort William after 1803) about the end of June (about 1800 miles from their point of origin.[1]) Meanwhile, at ice-out, other voyageurs left the posts in the west where they had wintered (some as far as Athabasca country) and worked their way towards Lake of the Woods, where they entered the Rainy River followed by Rainy Lake, Namaken, Loon River, Lac La Croix, Crooked Lake, Basswood River, Basswood Lake, Knife Lake, Saganaga, the Granite River, Gunflint Lake, Height of Land, Arrow Lake, Mountain, Moose and the Fowl Lakes, and the Pigeon River to Fort Charlotte, where they took their last portage — all nine miles of it — to Grand Portage itself. It just wasn't possible to make the journey from Montreal to the western forts and return in a single season. That is why there were two distinct groups of voyageurs: the "pork eaters" who carried trade goods from Montreal to Grand Portage (or Fort William) and brought back furs on their return trip, and the "hommes du nord" (men of the north) who had arrived from western outposts and would return with the trade goods to exchange with the Indians for furs the next winter.

Now it's easy to understand why the men of the west were called by their several titles: "men of the north", "Nor'Westers", "hivernauts" (winterers) or "coureurs de bois" (wood runners),[2] but why were the Montreal-based voyageurs called "pork-eaters"? The answer lies in one of the staples in the voyageurs diet — lyed corn boiled in a can of water, with a couple of spoons of melted pork fat added to diffuse the kernels and make a stew the consistence of pudding. It may also be that the term had reference to the fact these men enjoyed domestic meat all winter while the "winterers" in the west lived on wild game.

The "men of the north" generally looked down on the "pork eaters" and their occasional ridicule at Rendezvous sometimes ended in fights. For this reason, their camps were kept separate.

The annual Rendezvous lasted about two weeks, and it is a wonder the forts remained in one piece after the revelry. In fact, a jail was maintained for those who became too unruly. In addition to the thousand or more voyageurs, about twice that many Indians were usually on hand to join in the festivities. Of course, not all the time wasn't spent celebrating. The large packs of trade goods from Montreal had to be opened and repacked in 90-pound, canvas-wrapped bales. Furs were sorted, accounted for and again tied in bales for the trip east. Then, too, there were canoe and equipment repairs to be made. Grand Portage was also a canoe factory[3] with upwards of 70 of the birchbark vessels being constructed (mostly by the Indians) each season. Rendezvous time also meant payday for the men of the north. The "pork eaters" were generally paid part of their earnings when they left Montreal and the balance upon their return.

When the French chose Grand Portage for a trading post, they chose well. Over the years, all of the major trading companies had posts here: the North West Company, the Hudson's Bay Company, the XY Company and, in later years, the American Fur Company. All were relatively large operations. Macdonnell described the North West fort as including sixteen buildings. The gates to the stockades were closed at night and sentries posted — not so much to watch for attack as to be on the lookout for fire.

Located on a bay, the landing beach was sheltered by two points: "Hat" and "Raspberry". A small island, "Mutton" by name, lay at the entrance to the bay. It is the same today as it was then.

Contests of strength and endurance during Rendezvous often had a purpose. The nine-mile portage around the rapids and falls of Pigeon River gave ample opportunity for the men to show their prowess. Voyageurs considered this experience as one which separated the men from the boys. Wagers and challenges characterized the portage. Each man was expected to carry eight 90 pound bales (usually two at a time). However, as a bonus for anything over that load, they were paid one Spanish dollar per bale. A normal load of two bales at a time meant a total of 72 miles of portage, so the stronger men would try to take more. The record haul was reported to be a wager won by a voyageur who carried 820 pounds (more than nine bales) uphill for one mile! And the portage must have seemed all uphill since the spot where they came out on the Pigeon River is about 650 feet above the level of Lake Superior. Little wonder the only hazard to health more

Using a Tumpline to balance the load.

serious than hernia was drowning.

When the North West Company moved its operations to Thunder Bay in 1803, the Rendezvous traditions and festivities were continued.

The voyageurs, though small of stature, must have been remarkable physical specimens. Paddling from pre-dawn to after dark just had to develop tough arm, shoulder and stomach muscles, and the miles of portage surely made a difference in their legs, backs and necks. Neck muscles? True — the voyageur's neck absorbed some of the strain from the super heavy loads, because a head strap or tumpline (sometimes called a "portage collar") extended from around the forehead down over the shoulders and then the hips, trailing close to the ground. Cradled in the bottom of the tumpline was the first bale — tied in with smaller straps. Additional parcels were placed on top of the first and tied in place. In this manner the stronger voyageur carried as many as three or four of the 90-pound bales at a time. The men kept their balance by leaning forward and trotting at a fast pace. Passengers traveling with the voyageurs recorded that they were hard pressed to keep up, though empty handed.

The longer portages were traversed in stages. After going about a half-mile, the men set their loads down and returned to the canoe for the next load. When the canoes were empty they, too, were portaged. The smoke break or "pose" was the incentive that kept them going — it meant the only rest they would have all day except the stop for breakfast. The "pork eaters", with their huge Montreal canoes, had relatively few portages compared to the "men of the north"; they carried the canoes (upside down) with a four or six man team, two at each end and sometimes two in the middle. The smaller north canoes required only four carriers.

If you have ever portaged a canoe over a rocky trail with tangled brush that reached out and entrapped your ankles, with knee deep mud in the low spots and hoards of insects (mosquitoes, black flies, gnats and "no-seeums") that knew how to torment you when your hands were occupied — then you have some idea of what these men went through. Remember, too, the birchbark canoes were plenty heavy (500 to 700 pounds for the Montreal and 200 to 300 pounds for the north), yet extremely fragile even though lined with cedar strips.

From two or three to forty or more canoes traveled together in "brigades", through the northland and even larger numbers on Lake Superior.

If the voyageurs ahead of you were from a rival company, it was not beyond them to drop trees gleefully across the path[4] to make your job even more difficult and time consuming. After all, if you couldn't arrive at your destination by freeze-up, you had to go the rest of the way on foot or hope to trade with Indians wherever you ended up — that is if you could find them.

There was little time for frivolity on the journey, but there were special occasions. When the Grand Portage was conquered on the return west and all packs were at Fort Charlotte on the Pigeon River, high wine was traditionally broken out for a celebration. Then, too, if a "pork eater" happened to be along — converting to a Nor'Wester — there was usually an initiation ceremony the first night out. After the hazing, the tenderfoot was expected to supply a round of drinks and take an oath that he would never let any "pork eater" enter the north country without a similar ceremony.

Hopefully, there would be stopovers along the way for more serious celebrating and even dancing. If there were no women handy (and there seldom were) the men had dances of their own called "rounds" — not unlike those of Greek or Jewish origin — where men simply danced in a circle, sometimes with hands clasped or arms on shoulders, to the tune of a couple of men beating on kettles or whatever else was handy.

But the day to day routine of paddling and portaging was strenuous to say the least. Everything had to move at a brisk pace in order to make the winter forts by freeze-up. Those who traveled with the voyageurs and wrote of their experiences, agreed that the days usually began well before sun-up, often as early as 3 a.m., and normally did not end until well after dark — thus making a 15- to 18-hour day! Only extreme weather disrupted the routine. Paddling was rapid — 40 strokes to the minute and even faster. Portages, as we have said, were covered at a trot. When the going was good they made 60 or even 80 miles a day.

There were only two meals: the first, breakfast, customarily came only after three hours of paddling on empty stomachs; Supper was as late as 10 o'clock at night and eaten only after all daylight had been exhausted. The menu wasn't much to look forward to, at least not by our standards. One wonders how it was enough to keep the men going at their torrid pace. Listen to this recipe:

1 qt. lyed corn (or dried peas) (Lye was used to prevent spoiling)
1 gallon water
2 spoons melted suet or bacon fat
Boil for two hours or until it has the consistency of pudding.

Then there was "rubbaboo" — flour stirred into boiling water to which pemmican was added. If there was time or good fortune enough to acquire game or fish enroute, this was also added to the "stew".

Pemmican was a blend of dehydrated buffalo or moose meat and berries, dried and powdered fine and mixed with animal fat. At one time, when buffalo were still plentiful on the prairies, the Sioux and other Indians prepared large quantities of pemmican as a trade item. Many a white man developed a taste for it.

Then there was "galette" or unleavened bread, similar to the "bannock" prepared by the voyageurs of today. Water and flour were simply kneaded into a dough. If birds' eggs were handy, they were blended in. Small flat cakes were formed and then fried or baked by the fire, often on a rock.

Of course, if tragedy struck and the provisions were lost, the men had to live off the land or starve. Radisson — before the day of the voyageurs — told of warding off starvation by scraping the lichens off rocks and boiling them in water until they formed a dark, glue-like substance. Don't try it unless you're starving — you won't like it!

The greatest danger to the voyageurs were the rapids. Some were so dangerous the home office in Montreal forbade the men to run them. Yet, most voyageurs preferred to gamble with their lives rather than jog the miserable portages with several hundred pounds on their backs. Crosses marked the graves of those who gambled and lost. It is said that the banks of one of the more dangerous rapids were lined with thirty crosses, even though it was outlawed by the North West Company. The fact that the canoes were so fragile made the rapids even more formidable. Every canoe contained a repair kit consisting of several rolls of birchbark, wattape (twine made from the roots of certain trees like spruce), and cedar strips. If a canoe was destroyed enroute, a new one could usually be constructed from materials found most places in the forest in about four days. If the packs became wet, a halt was called to dry out the contents.

The canoes were a remarkable creation. No nails, just birchbark over cedar strips tied together with wattape and sealed with pitch from the pine tree or gum from the spruce mixed with a little fat and charcoal. Thwarts across the top of the canoe held its shape. Seats, if any, were narrow. The canoes used by the voyageurs were basically the same as those used by Indians for centuries — only larger. Whereas the traditional Indian canoe was fourteen or fifteen feet in length, the north canoe was 25 feet and the Montreal canoes were 35 to 40 feet in length. The latter could handle a cargo of from 5,000 to 6,000 pounds — including the crew of 12. The steerman or "gouvernail" stood in the stern and used a long, wide paddle as a rudder. The captain or "avant de canot" was in the prow. His paddle was the longest of all and was used to ward off rocks while going through rapids. The rest of the crew were called "milieu" or "middlemen"; they were the paddlers who gave the boat momentum. Their paddles were three and one-half to four feet in length and extremely narrow by today's standards — about three inches. The north canoes had the same arrangement but a smaller crew — eight men — and carried about 3,000 pounds.

Because of the fragile nature of the canoe, it could not be pulled up on the beach without first emptying the cargo. It was the duty of the "endmen" to jump into waist-deep water and stabilize the boat while the "milieu" did the unloading. Sometimes the canoes were left to float off shore overnight, anchored only with a pole with one end across the gunwhales and the other on shore. If there was bad weather at night, the vessels were emptied of their cargo and overturned to provide shelter. It was even more difficult to navigate upstream through shallows or rapids than going with the current. If they were deemed to be "not too hazardous", the men would pole the canoe or "track" it by leaving only the steersman aboard while others towed the boat from the shallow waters or from the shore. Even if half of the cargo had to be removed, it was worth the effort rather than portaging everything.

If there ever was a "super-voyageur", it was the Athabascan. Because he traveled so far, his challenge was the greater. Then, too, he had to overcome the 12-mile Methye portage just after leaving Athabasca and its famous Fort Chipewyan. The portage included a 700 ft. cliff which was conquered by using a sled-like contrivance to cradle the canoes. If the ice-out was late, the Athabascans could not make Grand Portage in time for the Rendezvous, and so for a number of years an "Athabascan House" was operated on Rainy Lake as their terminal point.

In the days before the merger, when the Hudson's Bay Company was extending its influence south from Hudson's Bay, the Scots and English used some canoes, but also developed their own kind of boat. They were wooden, double-prowed, oversized row boats which varied between 28 and 40 feet in length. They were named "York boats" after York Factory, the Hudson's Bay trading post where they were manufactured. Most of the men who manned them were experienced oarsmen from the Orkney islands off the north coast of Scotland (therefore called Orkneymen). Although clumsy in appearance when compared to the canoes of the Indians and voyageurs, they proved practical and durable on the larger rivers and on open waters. But somehow, the Scots and Englishmen who propelled these York boats lacked the color and romantic flair of the French Canadians with their swift canoes. In each case, the men and their vessels were well matched.

During the winter months when the "pork eaters" were enjoying relative comfort in their homes along the St. Lawrence, the "men of the north" were enduring the rugged wilderness outposts where many of them turned "trader" meeting the Indians at these outposts and exchanging the goods they had transported the previous summer for their furs. Trade goods included many things: guns, powder, shot, liquors, knives, kettles, other cooking utensils, sewing instruments, flour, salt, grease, trinkets, cloth, items of clothing and blankets. Most trade items were manufactured abroad: hardware and cloth in England, beads in Italy, wine in France and rum in the West Indies. The famous Hudson Blanket was a favorite and is still popular on today's market. The quality and size of the blanket was graded in "points". The points, in turn represented the number of beaver pelts which would be required in trade. Thus, a two point blanket was traded for two beaver skins.

The voyageurs had other winter chores — cutting firewood, hunting, cutting construction timbers, rendering lard from the back fat of animals and even erecting buildings. Sometimes entire forts had to be constructed. Grace Nute, in her book, *The Voyageurs*,[5] tells us that no nails were used; the logs were grooved and notched to fit tightly together. Chimneys were made of mud mixed with sticks or stones. White clay was available in some areas and used both as a plaster and whitewash. Oiled deerskins substituted for glass in windows, and although one could not see through them, they did admit light. Roofs were often made of thatched bows, but shingles were used on the more permanent buildings. However, the cabins within the stockades were not uncomfortable. Permanent forts had gardens; Indians were employed to supply meat; and hogs were even imported to butcher and eat on very special occasions.

Winter travel was difficult and usually on foot with snowshoes. The more fortunate had dog teams, and were usually supplied with animals from the Indian villages.

Most "men of the north" were married — often to Indian maidens — who impressed them with their small stature, soft skin and tiny hands and feet. The offspring of these marriages stayed on in the west to help develop that part of Canada.

The age of the voyageurs lasted almost into the 20th century. The coming of steamboats, ox carts, stage coaches and then the railroad made the canoe obsolete. The economy changed, too. Logging and mining were more profitable — particularly as furs went out of fashion in western Europe.

Gone is the voyageur, but his achievements challenge our imagination and inspire us to stretch our own personal performance in other areas of endeavor. The voyageur showed us that we seldom do more than scratch the surface of our abilities. We are tied in spirit to these vivacious little Frenchmen as we paddle the very same waters and tread the very same portages. What a privilege!

[1]There was usually an "R and R" stop at Mackinac while fresh supplies were taken aboard.

[2]Usually referred to unlicensed traders.

[3]Rainy Lake Indians were also well known canoe manufacturers and the trading companies purchased them for use by the voyageurs and traders.

[4]By 1803, there were so many trees across the trail it is believed to be one reason operations were moved to Fort William.

[5]Grace Lee Nute, *The Voyageurs*, Minnesota Historical Society.

CHAPTER IV
THREE GREAT
TRADING POSTS

Fond du Lac

It was the explorer, the sieur Du Lhut, who made Fond du Lac (the end of the lake) historically significant in his very first visit in 1679. It was here, you will recall from the second chapter, that the adventurous Frenchman gathered together representatives of the Indian tribes from a vast area—the Dakota-Sioux, the Assiniboine and the Cree. One wonders how he ever got the word out to the leaders of these tribal kingdoms and persuaded them to come to the conclave. Duluth brought representatives of the Ojibway with him — all the way from Sault Ste. Marie where he had spent the previous winter.

Duluth had an ambitious plan. There was an abundance of furs available in the western wilderness but a handful of traders couldn't begin to take advantage of the opportunity. It was his strategy to train the Ojibway to be his "middlemen" who would do the actual trading of goods for furs, and then bring the furs back to the French. It was a bold plan because it meant there would have to be peace among the tribes and the Ojibway would have to be welcomed in peace. But the plan apparently worked and there was relative peace for more than 50 years and this then was how the French procured many of their furs in the western Lake Superior area.

Duluth and his men continued their presence on Lake Superior through the 1680s with operations at various times at Thunder Bay, Grand Portage and Nipigon (1684). Pierre Le Sueur[1] followed Duluth as commandant of the Lake Superior region and he headquartered on the south shore of Madeline Island (1693). We also know that LeSueur operated extensively in what is now called Minnesota and western Wisconsin. He was particularly active on the St. Croix River and the Mississippi River and its tributaries via Fond du Lac.

In 1696, Louis XIV of France revoked all fur trading licenses. The reason given was that there was a surplus of furs in France. This proved to be a costly mistake because it gave the British a free hand. By the time the French wanted more furs they were at a disadvantage.

The French lost their posts on Hudson's Bay to the British with the signing of the Peace of Utrecht in 1713. This renewed their interest in Lake Superior and, as we saw in Chapter II, a parade of French explorers and traders accessed the wilderness through Grand Portage and the Kaministiquia River (De Noyon, La Noue, the La Vérendryes, etc.) There were French traders at Fond du Lac during that period as well.

The treaty which ended the French and Indian War and other French-British fighting in 1763 gave all of the Lake Superior area to the British. Thus, in 1765, an Englishman, Alexander Henry, was in charge of operations on Lake Superior out of a base on Madeline Island. He sent traders to Fond du Lac to establish operations there.

Perrault was one of countless Frenchmen who went to work for the British after 1763. He was employed by the North West Company. In 1784 he was at Fond du Lac and met with one of his company's traders there — a man named Du fault who had a wintering house on what is now Rice's Point (Duluth).

In 1789, Perrault returned to Fond du Lac along with six other traders. They planned a cooperative venture and established posts on Leech, Ottertail and the Red Lakes and Pine River — with Fond du Lac as the headquarters. This arrangement worked so well that in 1793 the North West Company directed Perrault to build a permanent fort[2] at Fond du Lac. He chose a site along Conners Point (Superior) about halfway between the end of the point and the mouth of the Nemadji River. He had a crew of 10 men. They worked through the winter and erected two 40-foot houses and a storage facility 60 feet in length. When it was done, he named it "Fort St. Louis". It served for more than 20 years as a major North West fort and was a central distribution point for the company's operations on the upper St. Louis, the Nemadji, the Crow Wing and the Pine Rivers and on Sandy, Cass, Leech and the Red Lakes, with occasional posts as far west as the Red River. In 1805, there were 109 men employed in the Fond du Lac Department.

There were also independent traders at Fond du Lac from time to time and during the short life of the XY Company, they had a post there operated by Michel Curot (1804).

Although Fond du Lac became American soil in 1783 following the revolution, the British (through the North West Company) retained a presence there until 1817. This is a little hard to understand since the British were forced to leave Grand Portage in 1803.

In 1809, John Astor's American Fur Company moved into Fond du

Lac and competed with the North West Company, but they decided rather than fight each other, they would be better off to combine their operations — thus forming the Southwest Company in 1811. Fort St. Louis was the headquarters.

With the outbreak of the War of 1812, the British military moved in and Astor was pushed out. The traders with British loyalties were given military commissions and directed to recruit Indian warriors for an attack on the United States from the west. Col. Robert Dickson was the best known and most effective of these traders turned soldiers. The Dakota-Sioux were willing but the Ojibway preferred to stay neutral. This had the effect of preventing most of the Sioux from leaving their villages unprotected from the Ojibway. A few Sioux did join the British, however, in some attacks out east.

After the war, the British military left.

In 1816, as we have already seen, the Hudson's Bay Company

The foreground is the site of the second Fort St. Louis — on Minnesota soil. The arrow on the right side of the picture points out the only building in the picture which was included in the trading post. It served as a business office.

captured all of the North West Forts, including Fond du Lac, where they continued to use North West traders. The H.B.C. officials left the following summer and Astor then bought out the North West operations (1817). This ended the British era at Fond du Lac, which included more than 30 years of illegal operations after the American Revolution.

Fort St. Louis was then abandoned and a new fort was constructed on Minnesota soil.

During the years that followed, the A.F.C. post was managed by two able and historic figures: first William Morrison (for 10 years) and then William Aitkin (for whom the city was named). Both men traveled extensively through northern Wisconsin and Minnesota during their administrations.

At Fond du Lac, in 1826, General Lewis Cass presided at the negotiation of the first Indian Treaty on what is now Minnesota soil. It was similar in content to the Prairie du Chien Treaty signed the previous year which pledged the Ojibway and the Dakota-Sioux to live in peace. Neither treaty was particularly effective.

Two well-known Protestant Missionaries were at Fond du Lac during this era—Rev. William Boutwell and Rev. Edmund Ely. Boutwell was stationed at Leech Lake but traveled the area and was married at Fond du Lac. When he visited the fort with Henry Schoolcraft, he gave a sermon to a congregation estimated at "400 whites and half-breeds".

Ely headquartered at Fond du Lac and was part of the transition between the fur trading era and the influx of white settlers. The Treaty of 1854, signed at La Pointe, opened the region to settlement. Ely was also on hand as the logging operations began. In 1839 he wrote of meeting a man named Boyce with a raft of logs at the mouth of the Kettle River.

Nearly 200 years of exciting fur trade history separated Duluth's first visit and the opening of the area to white settlers and the birth of the cities of Duluth and Superior.

Grand Portage
(the great carrying place)

Grand Portage may have been the earliest white settlement in Minnesota. There is good reason to believe Radisson and Groseilliers were here in the 1650s and Duluth in 1679. Others used the location as a base of operations from that time on. It is likely that there was a post on this site in La Vérendrye's day[3] (the 1730s); he was the first to make a written record of using the Grand Portage trail. The location on the largest indentation on the Minnesota shore of Lake Superior, adjacent to the trail leading to the *Boundary Waters* route, made Grand Portage an ideal site for a settlement.

The first British traders arrived in 1762 following the takeover of the region by the British from the French. In 1766 or shortly thereafter, John Askin is thought to have cleared the site for the construction of the great North West Company fort. Jonathan Carver visited here in 1767.

After the 1730s Grand Portage surpassed Thunder Bay as a center of trading activity on Lake Superior and the huge North West fort was constructed in 1788 (and abandoned in 1803). A replica of the fort may be seen today at Grand Portage. Several descriptions have survived of the fort at its prime. The stockade enclosed 16 buildings, the most important of which were painted or trimmed in "Spanish brown". Their roofs were of cedar or pine shingles, in contrast to the thatched bows used on more temporary buildings on the frontier. The Great Hall was the most important building and it was here where meals were served and the historic trading and negotiating took place. The gates of the fort were closed at night and sentries posted — more to watch for fire than some human enemy.

Great Hall at Grand Portage restored (1975 Photo)

Courtesy Minnesota Historical Society

Other forts and posts were erected at Grand Portage, particularly during its "hey day". We know that in 1802 there was a smaller stockade known as "Boucher's Fort" and the tents of the XY Company were set up between that post and the North West Company stockade. The XY Company also had a post near Fort Charlotte on the Pigeon River at the other end of the portage.

In 1800, the United States tax collector arrived and served notice that duty would be charged on goods brought in from Canada starting the next year. The British responded by moving their operations north to Fort William (Thunder Bay) and thereafter used the Kaministiquia River route to Rainy Lake. However, the British did continue some operations at Grand Portage until after the War of 1812 — on which occasion Lt. Thomas Bennett occupied the site with a garrison to protect it against a possible American invasion.

The voyageurs preferred the Grand Portage route. The more northern route had more swampy portages and a seemingly greater infestation of insects.

From 1802 to 1830, there were several small, independent operations here under license from the United States government. In the 1830s and '40s, John Jacob Astor's American Fur Company was on the scene but was more involved in commercial fishing (on Lake Superior) than fur trading.

In 1838, that spiritual giant, Father Pierz, started a Catholic school and mission here. In 1856, Grand Portage was recognized with its own post office. A wharf was constructed in the 1780s. Sailing vessels out of Sault Ste. Marie had made Grand Portage a port of call starting with the American revolution.

The Ojibway Village at Grand Portage kept itself quite separate from other Chippewa bands and over the early years developed close ties with the British, even after their trading operations were moved north to Fort William in the early 1800s. The village was ignored as the U.S. Government signed treaties with all other American Ojibway and it wasn't until 1854 that the Grand Portage Indians had their own Treaty. After that date they were more closely affiliated with the other Minnesota and Wisconsin bands and identified with the United States. The population of the village varied over the years. Schoolcraft reported 60 "some" in 1828 and 50 in 1832. By 1940, however, the community had increased to 135. Descendants of the original village inhabit the reservation today.

Although Grand Portage has been in use by the white man since the 1650s and by the Indian for unknown generations, the peak of activity was over a twenty-five year period during the last part of the 18th Century, when a thousand or more voyageurs and perhaps twice that many Indians gathered in Rendezvous each July (Chapter III). The arrival of the voyageurs must have been dramatic. It was the custom of the "pork eaters" to stop short of the bay and dress in their finest and most gaudy clothing. Then, with paddles swinging in time to a favorite chantey, they rounded the last point and approached the beach.

The setting was then much as it is now, the bay framed by two points, "Hat" and "Raspberry", with Mutton Island lying at the entrance. As the voyageurs entered the bay they were greeted by a panorama of bustling trading posts, tents and Indian lodges with Sugar Loaf Mountain as the backdrop for the great North West Fort. Since about 70 canoes were manufactured by the Indians here each year, there were probably several under construction at any one time to replace those battered by the rugged journey. It is difficult to imagine a more exciting or colorful frontier settlement. Grand Portage is a National Historic site and was established as a National Monument in 1960.

Fort William

The Sieur du Lhut appears to have been associated with early fur trading operations at the sites of all three of the forts discussed in this chapter. We have seen how he convened a conference of tribal leaders at Fond du Lac in 1679 and he is believed to have used, or at least visited, the Grand Portage site. He is also credited with constructing the first trading post on the Kaministiquia River at Thunder Bay near or on the site of Fort William; it was called Fort Caministigoyan. It is very likely that Radisson and his brother-in-law, Grossilliers, were here even earlier. They were on the lake in the 1650s. Because their travels took them up and down the lake several times, it is assumed they conducted business here, but we cannot document this.

De la Noue built a post close to Duluth's fort at the mouth of the

A sketch of the original Fort William

Kaministiquia River in 1717. La Vérendrye wintered here in 1731-'32 on his first venture to the Lake of the Woods.

The Indians used this route of travel of course for many hundreds of years before the arrival of the white explorers. Since it was called the "old Sioux trail", we can assume that even that tribe found their way to Lake Superior by this route.

The Grand Portage passage, as we have said, was deemed to be the better of the two routes because the portages were a little easier to negotiate and because there were fewer insect problems. The French, therefore, abandoned the Kaministiquia site in the 1730s and thereafter mostly used the Grand Portage route. The first major North West Company fort was built at Grand Portage in 1788. As stated earlier, once it was determined the fort was on United States soil and that government threatened to collect duty on all Canadian goods passing through (1800), the operation was moved to Thunder Bay.[4] The first rendezvous was held there in 1803. From that date until the merger with the Hudson's Bay Company in 1821, the North West Company enjoyed its greatest activity, All of the Rendezvous festivities and the day-to-day work of the traders and workers found in the descriptions of Grand Portage were transferred here. A sense of the significance of the fur trade in the development of Canada and the excitement of the operations may be achieved by visiting the restored Fort William.

When the fort was first constructed, it was called "Kaministiquia", but was renamed in 1807 to honor William McGillivray, an early commandant of the post who later became superintendent of the North West Company. He was a nephew of Simon McTavish, the first non-Frenchman to run the company. McTavish had moved to Montreal from Albany following the British victories over the French in 1760.

The training manual for interpretive guides at the restored Fort William points out that the fort had many roles in the operations of the North West Company, and lists the following:[5]

- the place for the annual meeting of Company Directors and partners;
- the Company's inland office;
- a warehousing depot for trade goods, provisions and furs;
- the transshipment point between Lake Superior and the waterways of the interior;
- a service center for manufacturing and repairing certain trade items and containers for shipping, storage and cooking;
- a center for building and repairing the means of transportation used in the fur trade including schooners, bateaux and canoes;
- an agricultural base to supplement the provisions of the company personnel;
- the quarters for lodging, provisioning and equipping North West Company personnel;
- the hub for their social activities and festivities;
- a fur trade post for the local Indian trade; and
- the center for the trade of the Fort William Department which included the region around Lake Superior and west as far as Lac la Pluie (Rainy Lake).

Northwest ownership of the fort was interrupted by Lord Selkirk's militant takeover in 1816[1] and ended with the merger of the Hudson's Bay Company and the North West Company in 1821.

The fort declined in importance after the merger as the new

company made their posts on Hudson's Bay the principal outlets for furs from Canada. The H.B.C. closed the fort in 1881. The buildings were demolished to make way for new railroad terminal buildings and shops in 1891. It was because of the railroad facilities that Fort William could not be restored on the original site but was moved 14½ kilometers up river from that location. The last original building, a storehouse, was demolished in 1902.

[1] For further information on Le Sueur's explorations, consult *Our Historic Upper Mississippi* by this author.

[2] It was customary for trading posts to be built as forts with stockades, towers and heavy gates. Rarely was there need for protection against Indian attack. The enclosure served more to keep out unwanted visitors and wildlife.

[3] Although when LaVérendrye was first there in 1731, he chose to winter at Fort Kaministiquia.

[4] The border was determined by the Treaty of 1783 following the American Revolution; so the North West Company got by with using their forts south of the border for about 20 years. In fact, The North West Company had, in fact, a presence at Fond du Lac as late as 1817.

[5] Training manual for Interpretive Guides at Old Fort William.

CHAPTER V
COMMERCE ON THE LAKE AND ALONG THE SHORE

As we have seen in earlier chapters, the fur trade industry dominated commerce on Lake Superior–starting with the visits of Radisson and Groseilliers, Duluth and the La Vérendryes, and continuing with the scores of representatives of the Hudson's Bay Company, the North West Company, the XY Company and the American Fur Company. For nearly 200 years the voyageurs paddled their canoes back and forth across Superior's treacherous waters, heavily laden with trade goods, on their way west to places like Fond du Lac, Grand Portage and Fort William, and equally heavily laden with furs on their return journeys to Montreal.

This is not to say there was no commerce on the lake prior to the 1600s. After all, the Indian peoples had lived and traveled on the lake and traded among themselves for several thousands of years before the first white man dipped a paddle in Superior's chilly waters. The presence of "free" copper on Isle Royale and on the south shore (Copper Harbor) greatly encouraged traffic on the lake. The fact that copper was available in such a pure form that smelting was not required was extremely important to the Native Americans. The metal could be readily formed into projectile points, fish spears, hooks, gaffs, tools and ornaments. As stated earlier, these artifacts have been found in even the oldest burial mounds in the region.

Free silver was also available but in smaller quantities on islands and along the shores. Early explorers found the Indian peoples wearing silver ornaments and jewelry — sometimes shaped as animals, cones, etc.

Fishing was also critical to the survival of the lake's early residents. Fish were easily trapped in streams and netted in the lake itself.

Starting in the early 1800s, commercial fishing became an important industry on the lake for the white men, and remains so to this day. The American Fur Company made a concerted effort to market fish in the population centers along the Great Lakes — particularly whitefish, which they called "the most desirable fish in the lake". The AFC schooners were used as much — or more — to carry fish as furs. AFC fishing camps were established at Grand Portage, Grand Marais, the mouth of the Encampment River and Fond du Lac. Independent operators along the shore usually sold their fish to the American Fur Company.

Commercial fishing continues to this day, but on a reduced scale. Tough Scandinavians and Indians have eked out a living in or near

Commercial fishing operation

communities like Grand Marais, Grand Portage (the reservation), Little Marais and Tofte. Whitefish and lake trout were originally the most popular, but the whitefish population and market has not held up well and the trout were all but eliminated from the lake with the coming of the sea lamprey in the 1920s. Chemical control of the spawning areas of the lamprey has helped a great deal and with a good stocking program trout have returned to high population levels — high enough so that limited commercial fishing is once again permitted. Meanwhile, herring became the most popular fish taken commercially. At one time, in the early 1900s, most of the herring caught in this country came from Lake Superior. The herring population fell off in the 1940s, but has revived.

Smelt first appeared in Lake Superior in 1946. The smelt population reached its peak in the 1970s with nearly 3,000,000 pounds being taken

Netting Herring, Lake Superior, 1940

commercially each year. There has been a steady decline through the eighties and there has been no sign of revival in the nineties. The most common explanation for the decrease is the introduction of salmon and the revival of the lake trout populations.

Now let us go back to the 1800s and take a look at the history of the development of Commerce on Lake Superior, decade by decade.

The 1840s

During this decade mining was added to fish and fur as an important facet of Lake Superior's economy. During the forties copper mining was a fledgling industry at best and was located on what is now the Michigan shore (Copper Harbor). Iron ore was discovered during this period on the south shore.

The fur trade declined but commercial fishing increased.

The first passenger ships appeared; railroads were not yet a viable alternative on this part of the continent.

The 1850s

Iron mining blossomed at Marquette and copper mining continued with shipments out of Copper Harbor.

Excursion boats and passenger ships became more common — particularly as the lake was opened to settlement by whites.

The Soo Canal opened in 1855. Prior to that time vessels (some as large as 3,000 tons) had to be portaged for more than a mile on rollers, pulled by horses or oxen.

The Treaty of LaPointe, signed in 1854, opened the American side of Lake Superior to settlement. Parcels of land were platted and recorded almost immediately — including the west end of the lake out of Fond du Lac, bringing the beginnings of Superior and Duluth.

A man named Godfrey opened a trading post at Grand Marais in 1854 and he became the first postmaster when an office was opened there in 1856.

1856 was a big year for development along the *North Shore:*

- The townsite of Buchanen (about 20 miles from Duluth) was platted and a post office established.
- The town of Burlington was platted on the location of present day Two Harbors.
- Beaver Bay was settled; it has been the only community in continuous existence since that time along the shore between

Side-wheel passenger ship used on Lake Superior

Duluth and Grand Marais. A sawmill was constructed here in 1859; it operated until 1884.
- The town of Saxon was begun on the site of present day Taconite Harbor. Earlier maps labeled the area as Two Island River.
- The town of Parkersville was established at the falls of the Pigeon River; it lasted for about 20 years.

There was more activity in 1857:

- A Federal land office was established at Knife River and a hotel, boarding house and a boat landing were constructed. Copper was discovered and mining began almost immediately. It continued off and on until 1929 but without any real measure of success.

● Flood Bay received its identity when a man by that name established a sawmill. In later years, log rafting took place here.

The 1860s

Commerce of all kinds increased on the lake in the 1860s, particularly during and after the Civil War, but most of the activity—including logging and mining — was along the south shore. Communities along this shore began to grow into cities, and so did Duluth and Superior.

Some of the small communities founded in the previous decade along the *North Shore* continued to struggle along but were to have no significant growth until the development of the logging industry in the 1890s; others were communities in name only.

There were some new, but futile, attempts at development along the *North Shore* during this period. The town of Montezuma was platted at the mouth of the Sucker River in 1860 but, like many platted townsites along the shore, was never developed. Secondly, there was the opening of a copper mine at the French River in 1863, but it was not a successful venture.

The 1870s

In 1870, Col. Wolesley brought his huge expeditionary force (1,200 men) through Fort William on its way to quell the Riel Rebellion[1] in the Winnipeg area. Their wooden boats were not meant for portaging, but the troops manhandled them across the portages anyway. The expedition had two important consequences:

(1) the rebellion was readily put down, demonstrating the ability of the British-Canadian government to enforce law and order even in the far off wilderness, and

(2) the need for an all Canadian travel route was made clear.

The decade brought the Lake Superior and Mississippi Railroad to Duluth (from the Twin Cities), assuring Duluth of future population growth and establishing its importance as a seaport.

The Northern Pacific Railroad followed, connecting Duluth with Brainerd, Staples and the main line to the west coast.

The Duluth Canal was opened in 1871. Prior to that the docks were on the lake itself. During this decade livestock, produce and lumber were the chief exports.

Passengers, including immigrants from Europe, began arriving at Duluth during this period. The journey from New York was begun by rail and continued by boat, simply because it was cheaper than going all the way by train — but many did that, too. Two of the author's

Scandinavian-born grandparents arrived in Duluth by this route towards the end of the century. Most immigrants then went by rail to the Twin Cities from where they disbursed to the fertile farmlands of Minnesota and Western Wisconsin and the Dakotas.

It was also in the '70s that a rich silver strike occurred on Silver Islet (Thunder Bay).

Col. Wolseley's Red River Expedition by Francis Ann Hopkins

Credit: Public Archives of Canada

The 1880s and 90s

These two decades were a period of constant growth — except for a national economic depression in the late '80s.

Iron mines were opened on the three Minnesota iron ranges (Cuyuna, Mesabi and Vermillion) and railroads were constructed from the mines to Duluth and Two Harbors.

Along with mining, the lumber industry[2] experienced rapid growth. There were sawmills at each of the communities along the shore and, of course, at Duluth, Superior and Thunder Bay. Rafting operations took place at the mouth of every stream of significant size and the rafts were towed to sawmills in Duluth, for the most part, but some went to ports in Michigan and Wisconsin. Some of the larger rafting operations were at the mouths of the Talmadge, French, Sucker, Knife, Stewart, Gooseberry, Split Rock, Cross and Poplar Rivers. Also at Kadunce and Silver Creeks.

In addition, there were rafting operations at several points and bays along the shore, including Stony Point, Larsmont, Two Harbors, Flood

Bay, Castle Danger, Little Marais, Sugar Loaf, Tofte, Grand Marais and Hovland.

At Knife River, Alger Smith and Company established a major logging operation in 1898. They constructed nearly 100 miles of railroad — just to carry logs.

Logs entering the High Fall of the Pigeon River by chute.

The Schroeder Lumber Company had a sizable logging operation at Cross River until the early 1900s.

Lumbering also became the dominant industry in the Thunder Bay area in the 1890s.

On Lake Superior itself, steel vessels replaced schooners and other wooden ships as the iron ore industry blossomed. As exports of iron ore, lumber and farm products increased, so did the population along the shore. In the 1890s, Duluth doubled in size.

Once the railroads reached Duluth, considerable Canadian Commerce bound for Winnipeg went first to Duluth by water, and then by rail to the Red River. This practice ceased, of course, once the Canadian railroads reached Winnipeg. (1900)

The 1900s

During the first two decades of the 20th Century, expansion of iron mining, logging and agriculture (to the south and west) continued, and shipping grew proportionately. Only lumbering had its peak during this time (around 1910). During this peak period, the logging operation at the Gooseberry River included two rail lines with the rafted logs being towed to Baraga, Michigan, and Ashland, Wisconsin.

A sawmill was constructed at Thomasville in 1907.

There was also some mining along the *North Shore*, but not for iron ore. It was done by the fledgling 3M Company (then known as Minnesota Mining and Manufacturing), which at that time was based in Duluth. They used abrasives in their early products and did some mining at Corundum Point and near Crystal Bay, where they also had a crushing plant. The materials proved to be poor as abrasives. The mining and crushing operations ceased and 3M went on to bigger and better things!

Among the events which stimulated commerce on the lake in this century were World Wars I and II, the introduction of taconite (in the 1960s), and the opening of the St. Lawrence Seaway in 1959, which brought ships from all over the world to what the Sieur du Lhut had called Fond du Lac — the end of the lake.

[1] For further information consult *Our Historic Boundary Waters* by this author.

[2] For a more in-depth description of the logging industry in Minnesota, consult *Tales of Four Lakes and a River* and *Our Historic Boundary Waters* by this author.

CHAPTER VI
SHIPWRECKS

The majestic, serene beauty of Lake Superior can be deceiving. A howling gale — too often without warning in days gone by — can turn the lake into a treacherous, pounding sea with ocean-size waves.

In recorded time there have been over 350 shipwrecks on Lake Superior[1] with over 1,000 fatalities. Since written history is only about 5% of human history on the lake, and because Indians used relatively small and fragile birchbark canoes, one could safely estimate that the prehistoric and historic death tolls could well total several thousands.

The explorers, traders and voyageurs also used birchbark canoes on the Great Lakes. Although they were usually much larger than those used on the portages (north canoes) west of Superior, they were relatively fragile. Sheets of birchbark were sewed together with cedar or spruce roots and sealed with spruce gum mixed with charcoal and a little animal fat. Even though lined with cedar strips, a careless move by a crewman could spring a leak. Only 35 to 40 feet in length, the Montreal's, as the larger canoes were called, usually carried a crew of 12 men and a cargo of up to 6,000 pounds. With this heavy load and being of fragile construction, they were easy prey to a storm. The only weather forecast in those days was good judgment based on experience that comes from watching signs in the sky. Even staying in sight of land — which they usually did — was no guarantee of safety. There were stretches of many miles without islands or harbors for shelter.

These freight canoes left Montreal each spring at ice-out, headed for Fort William or Grand Portage, loaded with trade goods. They returned with bales of furs secured from the "voyageurs of the north" whom they met in July rendezvous at the west end of Lake Superior. They traveled in brigades, perhaps feeling there was safety in numbers. Harmon reported seeing 100 canoes in one fleet. There was another report of 30 canoes and 300 men in another brigade (June, 1800). We have no knowledge of how many of these canoes may have succumbed to storm or reef. The journals of the Hudson's Bay Company (possibly the oldest corporation still operating in this hemisphere) tell of a Montreal-bound canoe that capsized in a storm on August 26, 1816. This was during the time of the hostilities between that company and the North West Company. Lord Selkirk's men (Hudson Bay) had captured Fort William in reprisal for the killing of his people in the "Seven Oaks Massacre". Some of the men in the canoe were prisoners being taken to Montreal to stand trial. Of the 24 aboard, as many as 11 may have drowned. Dr. John McLaughlin, remembered as the "Father of Oregon" was among those saved.

In addition to canoes, similar sized wooden vessels were used. They were called "bateaus". They were heavy and not meant for portaging. Another wooden craft called the "Mackinaw" appeared on the lake. Both ends were blunt. It had a rudder and one or two sails. It was 30 to 40 feet in length. A few schooners (about twice the length of the Mackinaws and of the type used on the ocean) began appearing in the late 1700s[2] and early 1800s. A 78-foot schooner, the *John Jacob Astor,* was launched in 1835. It was used mostly for hauling fish and furs. It came to a disastrous end in 1844 as it was completely destroyed in a storm at Copper Harbor. Fortunately, no lives were lost.

There are several significant historic events which increased the use of Lake Superior for shipping, and, of course, the more ships there were on the lake the better the chance of an accident—at least up until the 1920s when better navigational technology and improved weather forecasting made a great difference. These significant events were:

- The opening of the Soo Canal — 1855.
- Production of lumber and grain west of Lake Superior and the availability of eastern markets via the lakes. — from the 1860s and thereafter.
- Construction of the Duluth Harbor Canal — 1871.
- Discovery and shipping of iron ore (and some copper and silver) 1870s.
- The expansion of the network of railroads westward, greatly increasing the availability of grain, lumber and ore — 1880s.
- The opening of the St. Lawrence Seaway to the Atlantic — 1959.
- The development of a process for extracting iron from taconite — 1960s.

With the coming of improved navigation technology and the construction of lighthouses, there were fewer shipwrecks. Thus, the vast majority of wrecks on the Great Lakes were in the 1800s and early 1900s. We shall list only the major disasters in this chapter. Many other ships were driven onto beaches and even reefs and then pulled back out into deep water without significant damage and no loss of life. It is surprising how many ships even settled to the bottom (of course in relatively shallow water) and yet were raised and repaired to sail again. It is interesting but not surprising that most shipwrecks took place in spring and fall when there is more fog and there are more storms on the lake. Snow and intense cold made life-saving more difficult. In the list of shipwrecks which follows, you will find several dramatic stories of struggles for survival against tremendous odds. The details of the dramas of those ships that went down with all hands is less known or left to the imagination.

The wrecks and disasters, which took place along the *North Shore* from Duluth-Superior to Thunder Bay are listed in the order of their occurrence:

The schooner ***Chaska*** — August 29, 1871. It was owned and operated by the Merritt family of Duluth (later to become well known for their railroad and iron mining interests). It was destroyed as it was blown ashore in an unexpected storm while hauling rocks for a breakwater for the Duluth harbor. No lives lost.

The ***Lotta Bernard*** — October 29, 1874. A side-wheeler, it wallowed in heavy seas off Encampment Island. The ship was enroute from Thunder Bay to Duluth with two passengers and 13 crew aboard. It was caught in an unexpected snow storm with a strong northeast wind. The *Lotta Bernard* was apparently a very slow-moving vessel and the huge waves began breaking over its stern, threatening to demolish and flood the ship. In desperation, the bow anchor was lowered, bringing the ship around facing into the blow. However, the ship continued to flood and when it became obvious it would go down, two lifeboats were lowered. The smaller of the two capsized immediately along-side the ship; two crewmen were lost but six scrambled to safety and joined the seven others in the remaining boat. The now overloaded boat pulled away from the *Lotta Bernard* in a blinding snowstorm in total darkness, shortly after midnight. Somehow they survived the wind, cold, and snow and about noon the next day were thrown up on the shore at Silver Creek.

It is very difficult to understand how anyone survived, even after making shore. They had to be soaked to the skin. Ten of the crew started in one direction looking for help and the other three chose another trail. The larger group found an Indian camp and received food and shelter. One of the Indians went back in search of the others. He found one dead (frozen), but he found the other two at the creek where they had discovered the lifeboat in good shape. When the storm had passed, the 12 survivors proceeded to row towards Duluth. Part way back (at Agate Bay) they found a small fishing camp. Here they were fed and warmed. They then returned to their boat and rowed the rest of the way to Duluth — about 33 miles of rowing altogether! And remember, this took place the last few days of October and the first few days of November.

The **Stranger of Superior** — December 12, 1875. A 60-foot schooner with a crew of four, it was caught in a gale off Grand Marais. It lost its power and had no anchor. People on shore saw that it was in trouble and was being blown out on the lake. They took a large rowboat out to rescue them and almost reached the ship, but the numbing cold and increased winds made them turn back in order to save their own lives. The helpless ship and crew were last seen being blown away from land and out to sea — never to be heard from again. Legend has it, however, that Indians found pieces of the ship and frozen bodies on a far shore.

The **Siskiwit** — December 25, 1879. A steamer tug, operated by a fishing company, was in the process of picking up workers at the end of the season from Isle Royale and along the North Shore and was on its way to Duluth. It struck a reef near Little Marais, partially disabling the ship. Loaded with passengers, the captain deemed it wiser to return to Grand Marais than continue to Duluth. Having reached this haven, the captain then borrowed snowshoes and walked the 110 miles to Duluth! Here he reported the problem and then returned aboard another tug, the *Amethyst.* After reaching Grand Marais, the *Amethyst* began towing the *Siskiwit* and its 24 passengers to Duluth. About halfway home a winter storm hit and both tugs quickly became ice-covered. With the Siskiwit in danger of going down, the passengers were transferred to the *Amethyst* — no easy task on high seas. The *Amethyst* then ran for shore and was beached. One man was hit on the head by a falling smokestack and was drowned. The others (all 29) escaped to shore and walked — in 30° below zero temperatures — to Beaver Bay. When the weather improved, they took a lifeboat from the tug, borrowed another, and rowed to Duluth!

The **City of Winnipeg** — July 19, 1881. A 200-foot freight and passenger vessel caught on fire shortly after it docked in Duluth harbor sometime after midnight. The 18 passengers escaped but four crewmen died in the mishap. When it became apparent the fire could not be controlled, it was cut loose from the pier and pushed over toward Minnesota point where the fire burned itself out.

The **Isle Royale** — July 27, 1885. A small steamer, it developed a leak off Susie Island (southwest of Isle Royale) and went down as the crew escaped to the nearby island.

The **A. Booth** — August 29, 1886. It was first wrecked on this date, was salvaged the following year, and then — enroute to Duluth — struck a reef near Grand Portage and sank again (July, 1887).

The **Mayflower** — June 2, 1891. A schooner, heavily loaded with sandstone. It was approaching the Duluth harbor and lowered its sails. Somehow, in the maneuver, the cargo shifted and the ship foundered. The seas were reportedly not heavy at the time. A tug saved the three crewmen but the captain drowned.

The **Winslow** — October 3, 1891. A wooden passenger steamer, it was tied to the St. Paul and Duluth Railroad dock (in the Duluth harbor) when it caught fire. Soon it was burning out of control and had to be cut loose and pushed over to Minnesota Point where it would not endanger other vessels or property. It was a total loss but there were no human casualties.

The **S.P. Ely** — October 30, 1886. A 200-foot schooner converted to a barge, it was under tow by a steamer, the *Hesper* which was headed into Two Harbors to pick up some ore. Winds came up (estimated at 60-70 miles an hour) and the towline broke. The *Ely* crashed into the breakwaters. No casualties.

The **Criss Grover** — October 24, 1899. A schooner, it broke up on a reef near Split Rock during a storm. No loss of life.

The **E.P. Ferry** — January 28, 1900. A wooden tugboat, it was destroyed by fire in the Duluth Harbor. No casualties.

The **Sagamore** — July 29, 1901. A barge under tow by the *Pathfinder*, it was struck, in a heavy fog, by the *Northern Queen*. The *Sagamore* went down in 70 feet of water and three lives were lost. There was relatively little damage to the *Northern Queen* and the *Pathfinder* was missed completely.

The **Thomas Wilson** — June 7, 1902. A whaleback steamer, it collided with the *Hadley* just northeast of the Duluth Harbor and went down with the loss of nine lives. The accident took place in good weather and should never have happened. Reportedly, the pilot of the *Hadley* changed course without sounding its whistle. The *Hadley* hit the *Wilson* midship and it went

A mooring cleat on the wreck of the *Wilson* that lies about 1 mile from the Duluth Canal entrance.

down immediately. There was no time to launch lifeboats but 11 sailors were saved.

The **Belle Cross** — Spring, 1903. There are several versions of this story but the following is so detailed it seems the most correct. The

Belle Cross had been carrying wood poles from the Gooseberry River logging operation to Baraga, Michigan. It was returning at night in a snow storm. The captain supposedly was confused by the lights on shore and ran up onto a raft of logs, disabling the propeller. The wind then blew the ship against the rocky shore where it quickly filled with water. All hands escaped but the ship was deemed worthless and towed into deeper water and allowed to sink.

The *Niagra* — June 4, 1904. A tug, it struck Knife Island in heavy fog and sank. No lives lost.

The *Hesper* — May 3, 1905. The 250-foot wooden steamer was caught in a 60-mile-an-hour gale and thrown on a reef on the edge of what is now Silver Bay Harbor. No lives were lost.

A close-up view of the timber construction used in the wreck of the *Hesper* that lies off the Silver Bay public access.   Kent Nordell

The disastrous storm of November 27 and 28, 1905, was the worst in recorded history on Lake Superior. It came without warning in the form of a blinding blizzard with winds estimated at more than 70 miles an hour. Thirty ships were severely damaged or destroyed and 78 lives were lost.[3]

Most of the ships met their demise in the dark of night in intense cold, which, in addition to the blinding snowstorm made it most difficult for the crews to survive — even if they made shore. As we continue our list of wrecks between Duluth and Thunder Bay, those which occurred in this storm are preceded by an asterisk (*).

* The *Mataafa* — November 28, 1905. Because this was one of the most dramatic wrecks caused by the storm in the Duluth area, local residents named the storm "the Mataafa Blow". The ship had left Duluth on the 27th with a barge, the *James Nasmyth* in tow. The storm hit that evening when the vessels were off Two Harbors. They survived the night but made no headway. With the coming of daylight, it was decided to return to Duluth. The barge was let go and dropped its anchors two miles out and survived. The *Mataafa* headed for the harbor. Just as it was about to enter the canal, a gigantic wave lifted the stern so high that the bow hit bottom. As a result the ship swung into the north pier. It was then held midships for a brief time against the pier

The *Mataafa* foundering in the great November storm of 1905.

where it received a severe pounding. Finally, it was washed past the pier where it ran aground about 600 feet off the beach.

Word of the shipwreck spread across Duluth and hundreds of its citizens lined the shores — building huge bonfires to give light and to assure those at sea of their prayers and support. Many kept an all-night vigil.

Meanwhile, on the foundering *Mataafa*, the crew was in jeopardy. At the time of the grounding, half of the crew of 24 was in the bow and half were in the stern. Four of the 12 caught in the stern decided to make a run for the bow; three made it but one returned to the stern. The 15 in the bow gathered around their lanterns for warmth. The captain then had a better idea and ordered a bathtub hauled into the room and the ship's woodwork was splintered into firewood. The bathtub fire helped them survive the storm.

The nine in the stern of the ship did not fare as well. When the storm subsided it was found that all had perished — four of them frozen to the top deck.

The *Mataafa* was re-floated the next year (1906).

* The *R.W. England* — November 28, 1905. As the ship approached the Duluth Canal in the storm the captain saw that he was not going to make the entrance so he turned the ship around and headed back onto the open lake, but the ship could make no headway and was tossed aground, like a toy — stern first — on Minnesota point. No lives were

lost and the ship was pulled off shore three days later and rehabilitated.

* The **Lafayette** and the *Manilla* — November 28, 1905. The *Lafayette* was headed for Two Harbors with a barge, the Manilla, in tow. The two vessels were caught by the storm and thrown against the

rocks below Lafayette Cliff, six miles east of Two Harbors just off Encampment Island. The barge (the *Manilla*) was up against the shore and the crew scrambled to safety by climbing into the trees against the barge. They then went to the *Lafayette* which had foundered just off shore and were able to get a line to the crew

The fantail of the wreck of the *Madeira* that lies just off shore north of the Split Rock Lighthouse.

Kent Nordell

and then pull a heavy rope ashore. The men came in hand over hand but one crewman lost his hold and drowned in the pounding surf.

A fisherman who lived nearby walked the six miles to Two Harbors for help through the drifted snow. The day after the storm subsided a tug boat from that community rescued the survivors.

*The **Edenborn** and the **Madeira** — November 28, 1905. The *Edenborn* was towing the *Madeira* (a barge) near the location of the present day Splitrock Lighthouse when the storm hit. The towline let go in the early morning darkness. The *Edenborn* plowed into the mouth of the Splitrock River. One man was killed on impact. The remaining crew members remained safely on board in the bow of the vessel.

The *Madeira* crashed

The pilot house of the *Madeira* sitting upright on the lake bottom at about 85 feet.   Kent Nordell

against the base of Gold Rock just east of the lighthouse location (there was no lighthouse there at that time). It was demolished by the waves. One sailor perished, but the rest of the crew were saved when a crewman jumped to the adjacent cliff and then dropped a weighted line. With this he pulled up a heavier rope and secured it. Three men escaped from the bow in this fashion and five from the stern.

The *Edenborn* was later pulled from the shore and rehabilitated.

One of the anchor winches on the deck of the *Madeira.*

Kent Nordell

* The **Spencer** and the **Amboy** — November 28, 1905. The *Spencer* was towing the *Amboy*, a 200-foot schooner made over into a barge. Lost in the storm the vessels were extremely fortunate in that they were thrown up onto a gravel beach three miles northeast of the mouth of the Manitou River (off Thomasville). Local fishermen and loggers heard the warning blasts of the *Spencer's* whistle and with their help all of the crew escaped to the shore via a hastily constructed chair-buoy. The Amboy was destroyed but the *Spencer* was towed out from shore and back to Duluth where it was rebuilt.

* The **George Herbert** — November 28, 1905. The *Herbert* was a barge under tow by the tug, the **F.W. Gillett.** They anchored in the shelter of Two Islands (Taconite Bay) but sometime after midnight the line snapped and the Herbert was thrown against the rocks. Of the five man crew, two leaped to shore and survived. The other three chose to stay with the ship and perished as it was destroyed by the pounding waves.

* The **Isaac L. Ellwood** — November 28, 1905. The ship left the Duluth Harbor on the 27th, loaded with iron ore. It was scheduled to stop at Two Harbors to pick up a barge but couldn't see the harbor. The captain chose to anchor for a time but the ship took a severe beating and began taking water. He then pulled anchor and returned to Duluth. He made a run for the canal but the waves prevented a straight shot. The ship first ricocheted off the north pier and then off the south pier — losing plates both times — but it made it through into the harbor. It was quickly towed to shallow water where it was allowed to settle, but all lives were saved and the ship was later refloated and rehabilitated.

* The **Arizona** — November 28, 1905. We conclude the saga of the Mataafa Blow with a happy ending. As the Arizona approached the

Duluth Canal at the peak of the storm it reportedly was caught in the fury of a cyclonic wind and was helplessly spun completely around, but ended up with the bow facing the canal dead center. The ship made it through unscathed!

The **Elgin** — October 28, 1906. Another ship converted to a barge, it was being towed by the *Crosby,* a tugboat, into the Grand Marais Harbor. It suddenly sank and was broken up by the waves. There was no loss of life.

The **Troy**—August 11, 1906. The wreck in this case was not the ship but the interstate bridge between Duluth and Superior — which the Troy rammed and demolished!

The **Benjamin Noble** — April 27, 1914. The ship reportedly left Detroit overloaded with steel rails, bound for Duluth. Some said that the ship was so low in the water her deck was awash. It was caught in a 65 to 70-mile-an-hour gale. Just exactly how and where it went down remains a mystery, although at this writing there have been claims that the wreckage may have been found. According to testimony, its lights were last seen about 3:00 a.m. somewhere off Knife Island by the pilot of the *Morrell* which was following the *Noble* and another ship, the *Norwalk.* Although it was at night and gusts of snow would blot out the ships' lights from time to time, the witnesses on the *Morrell* said that it looked like the *Noble* was turning to run behind the *Norwalk.* At this point the swirling snow blocked the view again and that was the last that was seen of the *Noble.* Those aboard the *Morrell* were not aware that it had gone down with all hands until they had reached Duluth and the *Noble* was not there.

Another theory is that since the severe storm had knocked out the fog horn at the Duluth Canal and the lights on one of the piers, the captain of the *Noble* may have reached Duluth but decided not to try for the harbor and went back out to sea, thus explaining why the wreck has not been found along the shore. The pilot house and other wreckage washed up on Minnesota point after the storm.

The **Onoko** — September 14, 1915. It was the first ore carrier with an iron hull and the largest ship on the Great Lakes when it was launched in 1882. It left Duluth with a load of wheat on a relatively calm day. The hull plates under the engine room split open off Knife Island, and the ship went down. The 17 crewmen had time to escape in lifeboats.

The **Liberty** — July 16, 1919. A 97 foot wooden steamer, it caught fire in Grand Marais Harbor and was totally destroyed, but no lives were lost.

The **James R. Sinclair** — August 7, 1919. A tug boat, it was towing a barge through the Duluth Canal when it suddenly jack-knifed and sank. One man was drowned. The boat was salvaged.

The ***Harriet B.*** — May 3, 1922. A wooden barge under tow by the *C.W. Jacob,* was anchored in the heavy fog out of Two Harbors. It was rammed and sunk by the *Quincy A. Shaw.* No lives lost.

The ***A.C. Adams*** — 1922 or '23. The exact date it went down is unknown at this writing. Its wreckage was located in 1991 about three-quarters of a mile off the mouth of the Lester River. It was found while divers were searching for barrels of waste (feared to be hazardous) dumped by the U.S. Corps of Engineers. It had a wooden hull covered with light metal and apparently was powered by a single cylinder engine. The ship and its story are currently being researched.

Mystery Ship — 1920s. This shipwreck is hard to document but old timers along the shore insist that somewhere off Two Harbors a ship went down with a cargo of 40 Model T Fords.

The ***U.S.S. Essex*** — 1930. Actually, this was not a shipwreck. The old wooden naval vessel was scuttled off Superior.

We have not listed any of the more than 30 shipwrecks off Isle Royale. Since those islands are a part of Michigan, we have not considered shipwrecks there as a part of the *North Shore* story.

Remember that the wrecks described in this chapter are but a small fraction of the 350 plus shipwrecks on Lake Superior in recorded history.

With so many disasters, it is little wonder that there have long been myths and legends about unworldly powers at work on the lake. A 1992 television special even compared the mysterious sea and air disasters on and over Lake Superior to the Bermuda Triangle!

Inspite of this mythology, modern navigation technology and accurate weather forecasting have made it possible for us to enjoy this wondrous lake.

[1] Wolff, Julius F., Lake Superior Shipwrecks, Lake Superior Port Cities, Inc., Duluth.

[2] Jonathan Carver recorded that the French had a schooner on the lake in 1776.

[3] Wolff, Julius F., Lake Superior Shipwrecks, Lake Superior Port Cities, Inc., Duluth.

CHAPTER VII
ORIGINS OF
COMMUNITIES ALONG
THE SHORE

The Twin Ports — Duluth and Superior

The early histories of these two cities are so entwined it makes sense to speak of their origins in a single description. Both communities can legitimately trace their beginnings to the first visit of the sieur du Lhut in 1679, on the occasion of his historic meeting with the leaders of several Indian tribes from the region. The subsequent Fond du Lac trading operations were alternately headquartered on lands which later became part of the city limits of what is now Superior and what became Duluth. As described in Chapter IV, we know that traders were present on and off after Duluth's first visit and that the first Fort St. Louis was constructed in 1793. From that day forward there was a continuous settlement of whites here as well as an Indian village, which probably predated the coming of the traders. The Fond du Lac Indian Reservation is located 20 miles west of Duluth near Cloquet. There were large numbers of traders and workers here from time to time. Earlier, we told how Rev. Boutwell preached to a congregation of about 400 souls.

Although we have excellent records and fairly good descriptions of the fur trading operations and buildings, little is known about the first homes and where they were located. George Stuntz, an early Duluth pioneer, reported finding outlines of long-abandoned houses on Minnesota Point in 1852. He estimated that trees growing in the enclosures were at least 75 years old. Lt. Allen, who traveled with Zebulon Pike and recorded his visit to Fond du Lac in 1805, described "dwelling houses three and four stories high". These may have been barracks for the workers.

With the signing of the Treaty of LaPointe in 1854, the area was opened to settlement by whites and people came into the Duluth-Superior area almost immediately. Superior grew the more quickly and shortly after the Civil War probably had about 700 or 800 residents.

When Jay Cooke, the railroad magnate, visited the area in 1871 he reported that Superior had declined to about 300 persons and Duluth had "six or seven frame houses, a land office and a school".

When the residents of the two communities learned that Cooke was contemplating building one or more railroads terminating at the lakehead, an intense rivalry developed. It even degenerated to the name-calling level with the citizens of Superior referring to their Duluth neighbors as "cliff dwellers" and "hill climbers", while the Duluth folks countered with calling Superior residents "swamp jumpers".

When Cooke chose Duluth as the terminal for both the Mississippi and Superior Railroad (St. Paul to Duluth) and the Northern Pacific Railroad (Portland, Oregon, to Duluth), the future of that city as the larger of the two was assured. By the time the Mississippi and Superior Railroad was complete in 1871, Duluth's population had mushroomed to about 3,000. In the first year of operation, the railroad carried two million bushels of grain to Duluth for shipment on the Great Lakes.

The Northern Pacific came to Duluth two years later. In that year (1873) the Cooke enterprises collapsed in the midst of a great national depression, but the future of Duluth had been secured.

Both communities prospered in the late 1800s as lumbering came to dominate the economy. In 1892, the opening of the Mesabi Iron Range gave shipping another tremendous boost.

Meanwhile, the rivalry between the two communities continued as

Duluth Harbor shortly after the turn of the century. Note the whaleback ore carriers in the background.

evidenced by Duluth's proposal to build a canal into the harbor across Minnesota Point with opposition to that proposal by Superior. The latter city claimed that the St. Louis River would be diverted through the canal and the natural (Superior) opening to the harbor would be blocked with sediment. Nevertheless, construction was begun in 1870. Superior took the issue to the federal courts, and the next year was awarded an injunction to halt construction of the canal. The decision was made in the courts in Leavenworth, Kansas, and the news was quickly wired to the Twin Ports. The canal was nearly complete by that time and by accelerating the work it was finished before the court officer arrived with the appropriate document, five days after the decision.

In 1898, the U.S. Army Corps of Engineers improved the canal, widening it to 300 feet. The construction of the Duluth canal did not end the rivalry. There was intense competition for the grain trade in the early 1900s.

Superior was not always the loser. The Alexander McDougall ship-building enterprise (The American Steel Barge Company) started in Duluth but moved to Superior in 1890. The steel oreships were known as "whalebacks" because of their rounded decks which shed water on high seas. The vessels were cigar shaped and had bows formed like a pig's snout. Thirty-nine vessels were constructed; the last in 1899. The disadvantage of the design was the uncomfortable rolling motion of the ship. They were replaced in the 1900s by larger, more stable carriers. The last of the whalebacks, the *Meteor,* is on display on Barker's Island, Superior.

One has to wonder if a state line had not separated the Twin Ports, whether their history would have been different, or if they might even have merged into a single city.

Knife River

The River was named by local Indians for the sharp, knife-like stones imbedded in its banks.

Knife River, the community, is one of the oldest settlements along *the Shore.* A hotel, boarding house, boat landing and land office were all established here in 1857. It is also the location of *the Shore's* first newspaper — *The North Shore Advocate.*

Considerable prospecting for copper was carried on here from before there was a community up to 1929. In fact, copper was probably the most important reason the settlers came to the area. Actual mining operations, however, were not economically successful.

The first logging operations were in the 1880s and Alger Smith and Co. of Michigan located their headquarters here in 1898, including a

Knife River logging operations.

railroad with nearly 100 miles of track. Logging operations were completed in the 1920s.

Two Harbors

Agate Bay and Burlington Bay provide the two harbors which give

Two Harbors docks, 1912.

the community its name. The townsite of Burlington was platted in 1856, but did not develop.

Logs were rafted here in the 1880s and 90s and were then towed to mills in Duluth.

Two Harbors enjoyed a landmark year in 1884 when the Duluth and Iron Range Railroad joined the port to the Vermillion Iron Range. This made Two Harbors not only a major shipping port, but the railroad itself became a major employer. The impact grew as the iron range prospered and as the railroad, now the Duluth, Mesabi and Iron Range, expanded.

The Lake County Historical Museum, located here, was the dream of the late William Scott, an attorney and Two Harbors native. He has been given much of the credit for the museum's collections and its portrayal of life in the area before the turn of the century.

Two Harbors is the seat of Lake County.

Tourism is important to the community's economy today.

Beaver Bay

This little settlement has been in continuous existence since 1856. There were logging operations here in the late 1800s, and early 1900s. A sawmill was in operation at the turn of the century. Commercial fishermen have been based here most of the time since the community was founded.

Silver Bay

This community was created to serve the then new Reserve Mining Company taconite plant which opened in 1955. The construction of the highly innovative plant and the birth of an entirely new city caused great excitement in Minnesota at that time.

Iron mining had appeared to be a dying industry. The supply of high grade ore was running out. It was commonly known that there was a very large supply of low grade ore, called taconite, but it was not known how to extract the iron in an economically feasible manner. Dr. E.W. Davis, a teacher at the University of Minnesota, developed a process that worked. Essentially, the process calls for crushing the ore-bearing rock into powder and then washing this over magnets which extract the iron. The iron powder is then formed into pellets for more convenient handling and further transportation.

Silver Bay grew into a city almost overnight. Schools, stores, homes and churches sprouted like mushrooms. Nearly 6,000 people moved in. Many worked in the plant; others provided goods and services. Surviving "first residents" tell of the excitement of being part of a "brand new" community — without the shackles of tradition or set ways of doing things.

In the early years of processing taconite, the waste materials, called tailings, were dumped into Lake Superior. As a result, miles and miles of shoreline were colored "iron ore red". The conflict of environment vs. jobs eventually surfaced. The solution — after a rather long and emotional dispute — provided for dumping the tailings on land.

The plant has not operated continuously. Whenever offshore ore has been available at lower prices, the plant has been closed.

Little Marais

The translation of the French word, "marais", is "marsh" — hence: little marsh as contrasted with Grand Marais, meaning big marsh. When the first white settlers arrived at this site, there was already an Indian village here. Logging and rafting operations were at Little Marais in the late 1800s and early 1900s, and commercial fishing has been important in the 1900s.

The economy has become increasingly dependent of tourism.

Taconite Harbor

The name comes from the shipping of taconite from this port which has already been processed inland at Hoyt Lakes (by the Erie Mining Co.).

The town of Saxon was plotted here in 1856, but did not develop. The Two Island River receives its name from the two islands at its mouth: "Gull" and "Bear".

Tofte

The name is derived from the Tofte family, brothers who emigrated from Norway and began commercial fishing operations here in the late 1800s. One of the better boat landings on *the Shore* was constructed in the early years.

There were logging operations here in the late 1800s and early 1900s.

Tofte is the starting point of the Sawbill Trail — an important entry to the wilderness canoe area.

A U.S. Forestry office is located here.

Tofte is one of the focal points for tourism along Superior's *North Shore.*

Lutsen

Lutsen today is synonymous with skiing and tourism. The Nelson family developed the ski slopes and it was here that Olympian Cindy Nelson learned to ski.

As elsewhere along *the Shore*, logging operations (including rafting) were found here in the 1880s and '90s.

Grand Marais ("Great Marsh")

The first white men to settle at Grand Marais were traders, and it is believed they used the harbor as a base for their operations as early as 1775. However, it was not established as a village until nearly 100 years later in 1871. In 1854 the trading post was operated by a man

Grand Marais in 1894.

Courtesy Minnesota Historical Society

named Godfrey; he also became the first postmaster when an office was established in 1856.

Henry Mayhew and Sam Howenstine and their families were the pioneers who developed the village site and opened a general store; they also became the managers of the post office.

The community has been involved in commercial fishing from the beginning; but sports fishing now makes a much larger contribution to the economy.

Mining also had its impact and it is believed the famous Gunflint Trail began as a wagon road to the Paulson mine. Legend also tells us that the mining road was preceded by an Indian trail.

Logging and lumbering have been a major part of the economy since the founding of the village and they continue to make a significant contribution. The Hedstrom Lumber Company is among the oldest and largest operations of its kind in the Upper Midwest and Northwest Ontario. It does both logging and milling.

Tourism plays the most significant role in the community's economy today. In addition to the harbor and marina there is a large campground on the lake as well as numerous motels. Grand Marais is a favorite stopping place for traffic to and from Canada and the restored Grand Portage fort is just a few miles up the highway. Grand Marais is also the beginning of the Gunflint Trail, leading to numerous lakes and the Boundary Waters Canoe Area.

The Canadian Twin Ports of Fort William and Port Arthur

Present day Thunder Bay includes both communities; they merged under the new name in 1970.

Fort William was the earlier settlement. As reported in Chapter IV, the great North West Fort was constructed here in 1803, but there were earlier posts and fur trading operations which can be traced back to Radisson and Groseilliers in the 1650s, Duluth in 1679 and de la Noue in 1717.

Following the merger of the North West Company and the Hudson's Bay Company in 1821, the new company made Hudson's Bay the focal point for its operations. Fur trading continued at Fort William, but on a diminished basis.

White settlers built homes in the vicinity of the fort and the growing community became the center for mineral prospecting in the mid 1840s. A townsite was even surveyed. At this time only a handful of whites were still involved in the fur trade at the fort.

Mining prospects faded in the 1850s but the opening of the Soo Canal in 1855 piqued the Canadian government's interest in this part of Lake Superior. In the 1860s, it became increasingly apparent that a route to the west was imperative and that Thunder Bay was the obviously best access point. However, rather than using the fort on the Kaministiquia River as the point of entry, the town of Prince Arthur's Landing was created a few miles from the fort. A road was built from the new community to Dog Lake.

The need for a route to the west became more obvious in 1870, when Col. Wolsley and his troops entered the wilderness at Thunder Bay and experienced such great difficulties traveling to the Winnipeg area to quell a rebellion.[1]

In 1882, the Canadian Pacific Railroad was completed between Prince Arthur's Landing and Winnipeg. Large numbers of immigrant settlers soon moved through on their way west. It wasn't long before wheat raised on their prairie farms was being shipped east by rail and then by water to eastern Canada. The community quickly became a milling center. The name "Prince Arthur's Landing" seemed a little cumbersome, so the name was shortened to "Port Arthur".

In the late 1800s, the railroad began looking for a site for its service buildings and repair shops. Both communities wanted the development and an intense rivalry ensued. Fort William was the choice and the terminal buildings and shops were constructed there in 1891. Unfortunately for history buffs, the site of the old fort was deemed the best location and those buildings were demolished. This is the reason the reconstructed Fort William is not on the actual location of the original fort.

Port Arthur was officially incorporated as a town in 1884; Fort William in 1892. As stated at the outset, the two communities merged in 1970 as they had grown into a single population center.

A silver strike on Silver Islet sparked a mining craze that dominated the economy from 1870 to 1890. After that, lumbering became the dominant industry. Wood products and paper remain important to the economy.

During World War II, iron ore was mined at Steep Rock Lake (north of Atikoken) and shipped by rail to the port.

Thunder Bay's current economy is well diversified but continues to focus on grain, paper (pulp), wood products and — of course — tourism.

[1] See page 63.

CHAPTER VIII
THINGS TO SEE AND DO ALONG THE SHORE

Visitors to *Lake Superior's North Shore* need not be concerned about keeping busy with things to see and do. Even life-long residents rarely find the time to do it all! Just look at this laundry list of recreational opportunities:

More than a dozen state, national and provincial parks
Historical sites, museums, restorations and points of interest
Fishing Lake Superior, streams and inland lakes
Hunting, particularly deer, bear and grouse
Sight-seeing boats
Excursion train
Camping
Hiking
Bicycling
Canoeing — including access to the Boundary Waters Canoe
      Area and Quetico (Canada)
Kayaking
Bird watching
Art galleries
Drama productions
Golf
Casinos
Alpine slides and gondola rides
Rock picking
Shopping
Dining, specialty restaurants
Picture taking

Wolf Ridge Environmental Center
The Witch Tree
Winter activities
Cross-country skiing
Downhill skiing
Dog sled races

Sightseeing and just experiencing the environment is perhaps the greatest recreational opportunity of all. The scenery is truly spectacular — and so varied. The rocky palisades along the *North Shore* have been compared to the coasts of Maine and Scandinavia. Cliffs along Superior and the Sawtooth Mountains provide vantage points from which one can see forever. More than a score of streams, including 15 major rivers, cascade their way over rocks and rills down to the lake. The foliage provides a beauty all its own, particularly with the advent of fall colors. And wildlife — from the shy deer to the majestic moose — provide a special treat for the keen observer.

Don't even try to do it all in one visit. As you read about the following recreational opportunities, pick and choose a few, giving yourself ample time to enjoy each experience to the fullest, and leaving yourself many excuses to return again and again to *the North Shore of Lake Superior.*

State and Provincial Parks

Before starting up *The Shore*, there are two Wisconsin State Parks within a few miles of Superior one may enjoy — *Pattison* and *Amnicon Falls;* both feature spectacular waterfalls. There is also *Jay Cooke State Park* on the St. Louis River. The grand portage (4-mile) of this river around the falls and rapids is still visible.

Gooseberry Falls State Park, named for the explorer Groseilliers,[1] includes a spectacular section of Superior shoreline and the river has five waterfalls. A visitor's center is located there.

Imagine the historical setting. This was a logging center in the late 1800s and early 1900s. Two rail lines brought logs to the river. At the mouth of the river the logs were formed into huge rafts which were then towed to Duluth, Baraga, Michigan or Ashland, Wisconsin. This is also the site of the wreck of the Belle Cross in the spring of 1903.

Split Rock State Park features a picturesque and historic lighthouse which has become the unofficial symbol of the *North Shore.* It was constructed in 1910 because so many ships were being wrecked in this vicinity, including six victims of the Mataafa Blow of 1905. There is a spectacular view of the lake and the Minnesota Historical Society[2] operates an interpretive center featuring shipwreck stories, the operation of the lighthouse and commercial fishing history.

Tettegouche includes one mile of shoreline, a hardwood forest, four inland lakes and the Baptism River. The river offers good fishing for trout and the lakes have trout and northern pike.

The George Crosby-Manitou State Park includes the Manitou River Valley and Benson Lake. Backpackers may camp overnight. Benson is a trout lake.

George Crosby was a Twin Cities businessman associated with the milling industry.

Temperance River is spectacular in itself and the park provides opportunities for camping and hiking. The river received its name from the fact it does not have a (sand) bar across its mouth — as do other Lake Superior streams.

Cascade River State Park includes six miles of shoreline as well as the river. There are opportunities for canoeing and fishing. The Cascade has a fall run of King (Chinook) salmon.

Judge Magney State Park is one of the larger parks on the *Shore* — 4,514 acres. It provides opportunities for picnicking, hiking and camping — as well as access to the Brule River. It is named for a former mayor of Duluth and Minnesota State Supreme Court justice who was instrumental in establishing 11 state parks.

Pigeon River is the newest state park (1992) along *the Shore*. It includes one mile of river and a view of Pigeon Falls; at 120 feet it is the highest in Minnesota. The falls was the main reason the voyageurs used Grand Portage.

Middle Falls Provincial Park is located below the middle falls on the lower 21 miles of the Pigeon River. There is a hiking trail with a good view of the higher falls.

Quetico Provincial Park is west of Thunder Bay on Highway 11. It provides an entrance to the Canadian portion of the *Boundary Waters.*

Kakabeka Falls Provincial Park is located 18 miles west of Thunder Bay on the Kaministiquia River. The falls are extraordinary.

Historical Sites

The restorations of the North West Company's trading posts at Grand Portage and Fort William at Thunder Bay are "must" stops. At Grand Portage one may visit the restored stockade and buildings (including a gift shop), follow the footsteps of the explorers and voyageurs on the inland trek to the Pigeon River, hike up Mount Rose for a spectacular view or take a cruise to Isle Royale.

Restored Fort William offers a living history of the fur trade era with dozens of actors portraying historic figures. One may see Indians demonstrating the skills of their ancestors, help welcome North West Company officials and voyageurs arriving by canoe, or visit with craftsmen of the fur trading era. There is also a gift shop.

The Depot Museum at Duluth is one of the most interesting in the Upper Midwest or Canada. It features perhaps the best collection of railroad equipment and artifacts to be found anywhere. Rides on an excursion train are available out of Duluth. There are also museums open to the public at Two Harbors and Grand Marais. There is an historic maritime exhibit at Two Harbors.

The Duluth Canal Visitors Center is well worth a stop. Besides the historical exhibits there is a very good chance a large ship — perhaps from a foreign port — may enter the canal while you are there, causing the historic elevated bridge to be raised.

Barkers Island, Superior, offers many recreational opportunities but the whaleback ship, the S.S. Meteor, is a very special walk-through maritime museum.

The "Witch Tree" on the lake near Grand Portage, may be the oldest living thing in Minnesota. It is a variety of cedar tree no longer growing in the state. For hundreds of years, Indians and Whites alike have placed tobacco offerings at the front of the tree to ensure a safe sailing.

Fishing, Hunting and Bird Watching

Lake Superior, itself, provides some of the finest fishing available, anywhere. You don't even need a boat! Shore fishing is most productive at the mouths of the many streams. Trout stamps and a fishing license are required.

Charter boats and/or guide services are available at Duluth-Superior, Two Harbors, Tofte and Grand Marais. Every freshwater game fish available in the Upper Midwest and Ontario may be caught in Lake Superior — plus several varieties of salmon. Charter trips usually specialize in Lake Trout, Chinook (King) Salmon, Coho (Silver) Salmon and trout (both Rainbows and Browns). Part of the excitement of fishing Lake Superior comes from the fact that any strike could be any of the above. Smallmouth bass inhabit the rocky, shallower structures.

The major streams provide spring Steelhead (lake-run Rainbows) fishing and fall salmon runs — a few streams include a third variety of salmon — the Humpies (Pink Salmon). Brook Trout inhabit the streams with some of the best fishing to be found in the headwaters — including swamps and meadows.

Many of the inland lakes are stocked with trout, walleyes, bass and northern pike are common to most. Conservation officers are usually more than willing to provide information as to which fish are biting in which lakes. Of course there are over 2,000 lakes in Superior National Forest so it is hard to be an authority on all of them! Maps are available from the DNR which will help you find the 56 boat ramps providing access to water in the national forest.

Inland from the *North Shore* there is a good population of big game, including whitetail deer, bear and moose. The latter may be hunted only by those successful in a lottery held by the Minnesota DNR (currently every other year). Fall grouse hunting can be excellent — depending on the cycle. Spruce hens are to be found in the swampier areas.

This is great country for bird-watching, particularly during the spring and fall migrations. The shore is famous for its migration of hawks and eagles in late September and October. Some years there is a winter migration of Arctic (Snowy) owls.

Sight-Seeing from the Lake

Sight-seeing vessels (harbor cruises) are available out of Grand Marais and Duluth-Superior.

There are daily trips to Isle Royale from Grand Portage.

Public boat ramps may be found at Silver Bay, Schroeder, Tofte, Grand Marais, Hovland and Horseshoe Bay.

There are private ramps at East Beaver Bay, Grand Marais Marina and the Grand Portage Marina.

Remember to bring a camera; there are many photo opportunities.

Canoeing and Kayaking

Access to the world-renown *Boundary Waters Canoe Area* is available via the Sawbill Trail at Tofte and the Gunflint Trail at Grand Marais. Permits are required and are available at the National Forest offices in the two cities just mentioned. The BWCA includes more than 1,500 miles of canoe routes with about 2,000 campsites — all in a truly wilderness setting with no motorized boats allowed. These are the same routes as were used by the explorers and voyageurs described in the preceding chapters. Guides and equipment are available from outfitters — several along Highway 61.

Single day trips are also available. Outfitters often recommend the Timber-Frear loop and the Kelso loop out of Tofte or the Rose Lake Stairway Portage tour out of Grand Marais.

Kayaking is becoming increasingly popular — particularly on the lake. Equipment and tours are available at Lutsen.

Camping and Picnicking

In addition to the BWCA camping opportunities, there are public campgrounds at Duluth-Superior, Grand Marais and Thunder Bay and private campgrounds at Little Marais and Schroeder.

The National Forest Service operates campgrounds on Sawbill Lake, Crescent Lake, Temperance River, Kawishiwi Lake and Poplar River — all on the Sawbill Trail. Also Ninemile Lake on Cook County Road #1. All have access to water.

Four of the state parks have campgrounds: Tettegouche, Temperance River, Cascade River and Judge Magney. The Crosby-Manitou park offers overnight camping for backpackers.

Picnic grounds are available all along the shore.

Hiking

The *North Shore* is a hiker's paradise. Trails are available in all eight state parks and others are marked along the shore. Nearly all streams have trails — many offer spectacular views of waterfalls and rapids.

There are lodge to lodge trails in the Tofte area; overnight accommodations are available by reservation.

There are a few organized, guided hikes sponsored by the Superior Hiking Trails Association of Two Harbors (Box #4), MN.

Hiking paths are also available off the Sawbill and Gunflint Trails.

Remember your camera.

Bicycling

It is estimated that Lake Superior National Forest has more than 2,000 miles of backroads — most any of which can be enjoyed with a mountain bike. Many of the tarred roads, of course, would be fine for standard bicycles. Suggested tours, according to individual interests, are available at forestry offices or from equipment rental enterprises in Lutsen.

Bicycling is not allowed on designated hiking trails.

Rock Picking

The *Shore* is known for Lake Superior agates and for Thomsonite. The latter is a semi-precious, rare stone found between Lutsen and Grand Marais. Both agates and Thomsonite[3] may be made into fine jewelry or purchased at local shops.

"Rock-hounding" for either can be great fun, but be sure to ask permission before going on private land.

A good quality of amethyst[4] is found in the Thunder Bay area. There is a mine six miles from Highway 17 on Loon Lake.

The rare Thomsonite gemstone, characterized by eye-shaped markings, is found at Good Harbor Bay near Cutface Creek, five miles south of Grand Marais.

Golf

Superior — Pattison Park (9 holes) and Nemadji (27 holes).
Lutsen — A dramatic, 18-hole course with a spectacular view.
Grand Marais — The Gunflint Hills course features a scenic 9 holes.
Silver Bay — A 9-hole course in a wilderness setting.
Duluth-Superior:
> Private —
>> Northland Country Club
>> Ridgeview Country Club
> Public —
>> AAA Auto Club
>> Big Lake Golf Club (Cloquet)
>> Enger Park Golf Course
>> Grandview Golf and Ski Club
>> Green Acres (Lake Nabagamon, WI)
>> Lester Park Golf Club

Thunder Bay — several courses

Wolf Ridge Environmental Center

Located just north of Silver Bay with a distant view of the Lake and surrounded by pristine wilderness, the center offers residential environmental education to thousands of school children each year. Programs are also offered for adults and families. Visitors are welcome.

Casinos

Grand Portage Lodge and Casino
Big Bucks, intersection Highways I-35 and 210. (Cloquet-Fond du Lac)
Fond du Luth, Duluth

Winter Recreational Opportunities

Skiing

Some of the finest downhill skiing in the Upper Midwest or southern Canada is available at Lutsen, Spirit Mountain (Duluth), Mont du Lac (Superior) and Thunder Bay.

Cross-country trails are available out of most year-around lodging facilities.

The John Beargrease Annual Dogsled Races are held each winter between Grand Marais and Duluth. John Beargrease was a legendary mail carrier whose route was the *North Shore.*

[1] The English had difficulty pronouncing his name and finally called him "gooseberry".

[2] Because the lighthouse is located in a state park, visitors are charged a fee by both the historical society and the state park system.

[3] A translucent, basically white material appearing like "eyes" in rocks.

[4] A blue-violet variety of quartz.

ENJOY!